DUBLINERS

James Joyce

D1439592

SPARKNOTES is a registered trademark of SparkNotes LLC

Spark Educational Publishing
A Division of Barnes & Noble Publishing
120 Fifth Avenue
New York, NY 10011

ISBN 1-4114-0249-9

Please submit all comments and questions or report errors to *www.sparknotes.com/errors*

Printed and bound in the United States

INTRODUCTION: STOPPING TO BUY SPARKNOTES ON A SNOWY EVENING

Whose words these are you *think* you know.
Your paper's due tomorrow, though;
We're glad to see you stopping here
To get some help before you go.

Lost your course? You'll find it here.
Face tests and essays without fear.
Between the words, good grades at stake:
Get great results throughout the year.

Once school bells caused your heart to quake
As teachers circled each mistake.
Use SparkNotes and no longer weep,
Ace every single test you take.

Yes, books are lovely, dark, and deep,
But only what you grasp you keep,
With hours to go before you sleep,
With hours to go before you sleep.

Contents

CONTEXT

James Joyce was born into a middle-class, Catholic family in Rathgar, a suburb of Dublin, on February 2, 1882. The family's prosperity dwindled soon after Joyce's birth, forcing them to move from their comfortable home to the unfashionable and impoverished area of North Dublin. Nonetheless, Joyce attended a prestigious Jesuit school and went on to study philosophy and languages at University College, Dublin. He moved to Paris after graduation in 1902 to pursue medical school, but instead he turned his attention to writing. In 1903 he returned to Dublin, where he met his future wife, Nora Barnacle, the following year. From then on, Joyce made his home in other countries. From 1905 to 1915 he and Nora lived in Rome and Trieste, Italy, and from 1915 to 1919 they lived in Zurich, Switzerland. Between World War I and World War II, they lived in Paris. They returned to Zurich in 1940, where Joyce died in 1941.

In 1907, at the age of twenty-five, Joyce published *Chamber Music*, a collection of poetry. Previously, he'd also written a short-story collection, *Dubliners*, which was published in 1914. Though Joyce had written the book years earlier, the stories contained characters and events that were alarmingly similar to real people and places, raising concerns about libel. Joyce indeed based many of the characters in *Dubliners* on real people, and such suggestive details, coupled with the book's historical and geographical precision and piercing examination of relationships, flustered anxious publishers. Joyce's autobiographical novel *A Portrait of the Artist as a Young Man* followed *Dubliners* in 1916, and a play, *Exiles*, followed in 1918. Joyce is most famous for his later experimental novels, *Ulysses* (1922), which maps the Dublin wanderings of its protagonist in a single day, and *Finnegans Wake* (1939). These two works emblematize his signature stream-of-consciousness prose style, which mirrors characters' thoughts without the limitations of traditional narrative, a style he didn't use in *Dubliners*.

Ireland permeates all of Joyce's writing, especially Ireland during the tumultuous early twentieth century. The political scene at that time was uncertain but hopeful, as Ireland sought independence from Great Britain. The nationalist Charles Stewart Parnell, who became active in the 1870s, had reinvigorated

Irish politics with his proposed Home Rule Bill, which aimed to give Ireland a greater voice in British government. Parnell, dubbed the "Uncrowned King of Ireland," was hugely popular in Ireland, both for his anti-English views and his support of land ownership for farmers. In 1889, however, his political career collapsed when his adulterous affair with the married Kitty O'Shea was made public. Kitty's husband had known for years about the affair, but instead of making it public, he attempted to use it to his political and financial advantage. He waited until he filed for divorce to expose the affair. Both Ireland and England were scandalized, Parnell refused to resign, and his career never recovered. Parnell died in 1891, when Joyce was nine years old.

In the last part of the nineteenth century, after Parnell's death, Ireland underwent a dramatic cultural revival. Irish citizens struggled to define what it meant to be Irish, and a movement began to reinvigorate Irish language and culture. The movement celebrated Irish literature and encouraged people to learn the Irish language, which many people were forgoing in favor of the more modern English language. Ultimately, the cultural revival of the late nineteenth century gave the Irish a greater sense of pride in their identity.

Despite the cultural revival, the bitter publicity surrounding Parnell's affair, and later his death, dashed all hopes of Irish independence and unity. Ireland splintered into factions of Protestants and Catholics, Conservatives and Nationalists. Such social forces form a complex context for Joyce's writing, which repeatedly taps into political and religious matters. Since Joyce spent little of his later life in Ireland, he did not witness such debates firsthand. However, despite living on the continent, Joyce retained his artistic interest in the city and country of his birth and ably articulated the Irish experience in his writings.

Dubliners contains fifteen portraits of life in the Irish capital. Joyce focuses on children and adults who skirt the middle class, such as housemaids, office clerks, music teachers, students, shop girls, swindlers, and out-of-luck businessmen. Joyce envisioned his collection as a looking glass with which the Irish could observe and study themselves. In most of the stories, Joyce uses a detached but highly perceptive narrative voice that displays these lives to the reader in precise detail. Rather than present intricate dramas with complex plots, these stories sketch daily situations in which not much seems to happen—a boy visits a bazaar, a woman buys sweets for holiday festivities, a man reunites with an old friend over a few drinks. Though these events may not appear profound, the characters' intensely personal and often tragic revelations certainly are. The stories in *Dubliners* peer into the homes, hearts, and minds of people whose lives connect and intermingle through the shared space and spirit of Dublin. A character from one story will mention the name of a character in another story, and stories often have settings that appear in other stories. Such subtle connections create a sense of shared experience and evoke a map of Dublin life that Joyce would return to again and again in his later works.

Plot Overview

"The Sisters"

A boy grapples with the death of a priest, Father Flynn. With his aunt, the boy views the corpse and visits with the priest's mourning sisters. As the boy listens, the sisters explain Father Flynn's death to the aunt and share thoughts about Father Flynn's increasingly strange behavior.

"An Encounter"

Fed up with the restraints of school and inspired by adventure stories, two boys skip their classes to explore Dublin. After walking around the city for a while, the unnamed narrator and his friend, Mahony, eventually rest in a field. A strange old man approaches and talks to them, and his sexual innuendos make the narrator uncomfortable. Ultimately, the narrator and Mahony manage to escape.

"Araby"

A young boy falls in love with his neighbor Mangan's sister. He spends his time watching her from his house or thinking about her. He and the girl finally talk, and she suggests that he visit a bazaar called Araby, which she cannot attend. The boy plans to go and purchase something for the girl, but he arrives late and buys nothing.

"Eveline"

A young woman, Eveline, sits in her house and reviews her decision to elope with her lover, Frank, to Argentina. Eveline wonders if she has made the correct choice to leave her home and family. As the moment of departure approaches, she reaffirms her decision, but changes her mind at the docks and abandons Frank.

"After the Race"

Jimmy Doyle spends an evening and night with his well-connected foreign friends after watching a car race outside of Dublin. Upon returning to the city, they meet for a fancy meal and then spend hours drinking, dancing, and playing card games. Intoxicated and infatuated with the wealth and prestige of his companions, Jimmy ends the celebrations broke.

"Two Gallants"

Lenehan and Corley walk through Dublin and discuss their plot to swindle a housemaid who works at a wealthy residence. Corley meets with the girl while Lenehan drifts through the city and eats a cheap meal. Later in the night Lenehan goes to the residence as planned and sees the girl retrieve something from the house for Corley. Finally Corley reveals to Lenehan that she procured a gold coin for him.

"The Boarding House"

In the boarding house that she runs, Mrs. Mooney observes the courtship between her daughter, Polly, and a tenant, Mr. Doran. Mrs. Mooney intercedes only when she knows Mr. Doran must propose to Polly, and she schedules a meeting with Mr. Doran to discuss his intentions. Mr. Doran anxiously anticipates the conversation and the potential lifestyle change that awaits him. He resolves that he must marry Polly.

"A Little Cloud"

One evening after work Little Chandler reunites with his old friend, Gallaher. Little Chandler aspires to be a poet, and hearing about Gallaher's career in London makes Little Chandler envious and determined to change his life. Little Chandler imagines freedom from his wife and child, but he feels ashamed about his thoughts and accepts his situation.

"COUNTERPARTS"

After an infuriating day at work, Farrington embarks on an evening of drinking with his friends. Even though Farrington pawns his watch to replenish his empty wallet, he finds himself spending all of his money on drinks for himself and his companions. Growing more and more frustrated, Farrington almost explodes when he loses an arm-wrestling match. At home later that night, Farrington vents his anger by beating his son.

"CLAY"

On Halloween night, Maria oversees festivities at the charity where she works. Afterward, she travels to the home of Joe Donnelly, whom she nursed when he was a boy. Along the way Maria purchases sweets and cakes for Joe's family. When she arrives at the house, she realizes she has somehow lost the special plum cake she'd bought. After talking, eating, and playing Halloween games, Maria sings a song for the Donnellys.

"A PAINFUL CASE"

Mr. Duffy develops a relationship with Mrs. Sinico at a concert in Dublin. The two meet often for long chats and become close, but Mr. Duffy cuts off the relationship when Mrs. Sinico makes the intimate but chaste gesture of taking Mr. Duffy's hand and putting it against her cheek. Four years later, Mr. Duffy reads in a newspaper that Mrs. Sinico has died in a train accident. He feels angry, sad, and uneasy as he remembers her, and he finally realizes he lost perhaps his only chance for love.

"IVY DAY IN THE COMMITTEE ROOM"

A group of men working as street promoters for a mayoral candidate meet to discuss their jobs and escape from the rainy weather on Ivy Day, which commemorates the death of Charles Stuart Parnell, the influential Irish politician. The men complain about their late paychecks and debate politics. Conversation eventually turns to Parnell and his political endeavors, and one of the men, Hynes, recites a poem he wrote in memory of him.

"A MOTHER"

An Irish cultural society organizes a concert series with the help of Mrs. Kearney, the mother of one of the performers. Mrs. Kearney secures a contract with the society's secretary, Mr. Holohan, so that her daughter is ensured payment for her piano accompaniment. A series of logistical changes and failed expectations infuriate Mrs. Kearney, and she hounds the officers of the society for the money, making a spectacle of herself and her daughter.

"GRACE"

After an embarrassing public accident, Tom Kernan is convinced by his friends to attend a Catholic retreat. The men hope that this event will help Mr. Kernan reform his problematic, alcoholic lifestyle. At the service, the presiding priest preaches about the need for the admission of sins and the ability of all people to attain forgiveness through God's grace.

"THE DEAD"

With his wife, Gretta, Gabriel Conroy attends the annual dancing party hosted by his two aging aunts, Julia and Kate Morkan, and their niece, Mary Jane. At the party, Gabriel experiences some uncomfortable confrontations. He makes a personal comment to Lily, the housemaid, that provokes a sharp reply, and during a dance he endures the taunts of his partner, Miss Ivors. Finally, Gabriel sees Gretta enraptured by a song sung toward the end of the party. Later, he learns that she was thinking of a former lover who had died for her. He sadly contemplates his life.

CHARACTER LIST

"THE SISTERS"

"The Sisters" narrator The reserved and contemplative boy who deals with the death of his friend, Father Flynn. The narrator avoids showing outward emotions to his family members, but he devotes his thoughts to the priest's memory. Others in the story see the narrator's relationship with the priest as inappropriate and exploitative, and the narrator himself seems unsure of what the priest meant to him.

Father Flynn The priest who dies in "The Sisters." Father Flynn's ambiguous presence in the story as a potential child molester initiates a book-long critique of religious leaders, consistently portraying them as incompetent.

Old Cotter The family friend in "The Sisters" who informs the narrator of Father Flynn's death. Old Cotter voices concern about the priest's intentions with the narrator, but he avoids making any direct statements.

"AN ENCOUNTER"

"An Encounter" narrator The young boy who endures an awkward conversation with a perverted old man while skipping school. Bored with the drudgery of lessons, the narrator dreams of escape. When imaginary games fail to fulfill his yearning for adventure, he embarks on a real one with his friend Mahony by skipping school and spending the day in Dublin, only to encounter fear.

Mahony The narrator's companion in "An Encounter." When Mahony and the narrator rest in a field, a strange old man approaches them. At one point Mahony runs away after a cat, leaving the narrator and the old man alone.

"ARABY"

"Araby" narrator The amorous boy who devotes himself to his neighbor Mangan's sister. Images and thoughts of the girl subsume the narrator's days, but when he finally speaks to her it is brief and awkward. When Mangan's sister tells the narrator about a bazaar called Araby, the narrator decides to go there and buy something for her. However, he arrives at the bazaar too late and buys nothing. The narrator illustrates the joys and frustrations of young love. His inability to pursue his desires angers him.

Mangan's sister The love interest in "Araby." Mangan's sister mentions the Araby bazaar to the narrator, prompting him to travel there. She suggests the familiarity of Dublin, as well as the hope of love and the exotic appeal of new places.

"EVELINE"

Eveline The protagonist of the story that shares her name. Eveline makes a bold and exciting decision to elope to Argentina with her lover, Frank, but ultimately shrinks away from it, excluding herself from love. Her constant review of the pros and cons of her decision demonstrates her willingness to please everyone but herself, and her final resolve to stay in Dublin with her family casts her as a woman trapped in domestic and familiar duties and afraid to embrace the unpredictable.

"AFTER THE RACE"

Jimmy Doyle The upwardly mobile protagonist of "After the Race." Infatuated with the prestige of his friends and giddy about his inclusion in such high-society circles, Jimmy conducts a life of facile whims and excessive expenditure.

"TWO GALLANTS"

Lenehan One half of the pair of swindlers in "Two Gallants." Lenehan exudes energy and exhaustion at once. He excitedly partakes in the exploits of his friend Corley but also laments the aimlessness of his hard living and lack of stability. Though he yearns to settle down, he remains fixed to Corley's side as the stereotypical sidekick.

Corley The scheming friend of Lenehan in "Two Gallants." Corley's bulky, assertive physical presence matches his grandiose bragging and incessant self-promotion. A police informant and skilled in taking advantage of women, Corley provides one of the most critical and unsympathetic portraits of betrayal in *Dubliners* when he dupes the housemaid into giving him a gold coin.

"THE BOARDING HOUSE"

Mrs. Mooney The proprietor and mother from "The Boarding House." Separated from her husband and the owner of a business, Mrs. Mooney firmly governs her own life, as well as her daughter Polly's. Her apparently successful plan to secure her daughter in a comfortable marriage makes her a morally ambiguous character. She demands equal treatment for men and women but also manipulates relationships to rid herself of her daughter.

Mr. Doran The lover of Mrs. Mooney's daughter Polly in "The Boarding House." A successful clerk, Mr. Doran fears his affair with the unpolished daughter will tarnish his reputation and bemoans the restraints of marriage, but he resolves to marry her out of social necessity and fear.

"A Little Cloud"

Gallaher Little Chandler's old friend who visits Dublin in "A Little Cloud." For Little Chandler, Gallaher represents all that is enticing and desirable: success in England, a writing career, foreign travel, and laid-back ease with women. His gruff manners and forthright behavior contrast with Little Chandler's delicacy.

Little Chandler The unhappy and fastidious clerk who reunites with his friend Gallaher in "A Little Cloud." Little Chandler's physical attributes match his name—he is small, fragile, and delicately groomed. His tendency to suppress his poetic desires suggests that he also earns his title by living quietly and without passion. He fleetingly rebels against his domestic life after hearing about Gallaher's exciting life, then shamefully re-embraces it.

"Counterparts"

Farrington The burly and aggressive copy clerk and protagonist in "Counterparts." With his wine-red face and fuming temper, Farrington moves through Dublin as a time bomb of rage. Farrington's job dooms him to unthinkingly repeat his actions, and he transfers his frustrations from one experience to the next without discernment. His outlets in life are drinking and fighting, a physical engagement with the world that typifies his lack of care and thought. Farrington's son is one victim of his rage.

Mr. Alleyne Farrington's boss in "Counterparts." Exasperated by Farrington's poor work, Mr. Alleyne yells at and insults Farrington until Farrington embarrasses him in front of the office staff. He serves mainly to exacerbate Farrington's frustrations and fuel his anger.

"CLAY"

Maria The quiet and prim maid and protagonist from "Clay" who goes to visit Joe Donnelly, the man she nursed when he was a boy. Maria is precise and dedicated to detail. She moves through most of the narrative with content satisfaction and laughter. Her happiness, however, faces challenges in the smallest of events, and her disproportionate reactions to small troubles suggest a remote detachment from life.

Joe Donnelly The man Maria visits in "Clay." Joe's brief appearance in the story provides a backdrop for Maria's own concerns. Like her, he worries about mundane details, but he also hides a deeper wound that the story does not articulate. He therefore serves as a sad figure of unhappiness.

"A PAINFUL CASE"

Mr. Duffy A solitary and obsessive man who eschews intimacy with Mrs. Sinico in "A Painful Case." Disdainful of excess and tightly self-regulated, Mr. Duffy lives according to mundane routine, and when a relationship evolves beyond his comfort level, he squelches it. His remorse over Mrs. Sinico's death makes him realize that his pursuit of order and control has led only to loneliness. He is one of the most tragic protagonists of *Dubliners*.

Mrs. Sinico Mr. Duffy's companion in "A Painful Case." After being shunned by him, Mrs. Sinico becomes an alcoholic and dies when she is hit by a train. She once grasped Mr. Duffy's hand and held it to her cheek, and this small, affectionate gesture led to the end of their relationship.

"IVY DAY IN THE COMMITTEE ROOM"

Mat O'Connor One of the political workers from "Ivy Day in the Committee Room." Quiet and reserved, O'Connor paces the men's conversation by tempering conflict and praise about the dead politician Parnell, but he shows little interest in his own political work.

Joe Hynes Reads the poem about Parnell in "Ivy Day in the Committee Room." Some of the men are hesitant about his presence in the room because Hynes is critical of the candidate for whom they work, but Hynes never wavers in his statements or views.

John Henchy The equivocating political promoter from "Ivy Day in the Committee Room." Henchy suspects everyone of betrayal. He suspects his boss of shirking the men out of beer and paychecks, and he suspects Hynes of informing the opposing candidate. However, he is the most equivocal figure in the story and constantly changes his own views to suit the context.

"A MOTHER"

Mrs. Kearney The commanding protagonist of "A Mother." One of the four female protagonists in *Dubliners*, Mrs. Kearney is ambitious but also haughty. She orchestrates her daughter's upbringing as an exemplary proponent of Irish culture and poise, but she has trouble dealing with Dubliners of different backgrounds and any challenges to her authority.

Mr. Holohan The befuddled secretary who organizes the musical concerts in "A Mother." Mr. Holohan is the subject of Mrs. Kearney's abuse, and though he remains quiet throughout the story, he is the only character who resists and counters her critiques.

"GRACE"

Tom Kernan The out-of-luck businessman of "Grace." After a
nasty, drunken fall, Kernan joins his friends in an
attempt to reform his life. He remains silent about his
accident, never questioning the men who were his
companions that night. His accepting attitude leads
him to go along with his friends' plan to attend a
Catholic retreat, but he never makes an active decision.

Jack Power Kernan's friend in "Grace." Power rescues Kernan
after his accident and suggests the Catholic retreat. Mr.
Power's dedication to Kernan appears shallow despite
his efforts to reform the man, as he is acutely aware of
Kernan's dwindling social status in comparison to his
own burgeoning career.

"THE DEAD"

Gabriel Conroy The protagonist from "The Dead." A university-
educated teacher and writer, Gabriel struggles with
simple social situations and conversations, and
straightforward questions catch him off guard. He feels
out of place due to his highbrow literary endeavors. His
aunts, Julia and Kate Morkan, turn to him to perform
the traditionally male activities of carving the goose
and delivering a speech at their annual celebration.
Gabriel represents a force of control in the story, but his
wife Gretta's fond and sad recollections of a former
devoted lover make him realize he has little grasp on his
life and that his marriage lacks true love.

Gretta Conroy Gabriel's wife in "The Dead." Gretta plays a
relatively minor role for most of the story, until the
conclusion where she is the focus of Gabriel's thoughts
and actions. She appears mournful and distant when a
special song is sung at the party, and she later plunges

into despair when she tells Gabriel the story of her childhood love, Michael Furey. Her pure intentions and loyalty to this boy unnerve Gabriel and generate his despairing thoughts about life and death.

Lily   The housemaid to the Morkan sisters who rebukes Gabriel in "The Dead."

Molly Ivors The nationalist woman who teases Gabriel during a dance in "The Dead."

Julia Morkan One of the aging sisters who throw an annual dance party in "The Dead." Julia has a grey and sullen appearance that combines with her remote, wandering behavior to make her a figure sapped of life.

Kate Morkan One of the aging sisters who throw an annual dance party in "The Dead." Kate is vivacious but constantly worries about her sister, Julia, and the happiness of the guests.

Michael Furey Gretta Conroy's childhood love in "The Dead" who died for her long ago.

Analysis of Major Characters

Gabriel Conroy, "The Dead"

Gabriel is the last protagonist of *Dubliners*, and he embodies many of the traits introduced and explored in characters from earlier stories, including short temper, acute class consciousness, social awkwardness, and frustrated love. Gabriel has many faces. To his aging aunts, he is a loving family man, bringing his cheerful presence to the party and performing typically masculine duties such as carving the goose. With other female characters, such as Miss Ivors, Lily the housemaid, and his wife, Gretta, he is less able to forge a connection, and his attempts often become awkward, and even offensive. With Miss Ivors, he stumbles defensively through a conversation about his plans to go on a cycling tour, and he offends Lily when he teases her about having a boyfriend. Gretta inspires fondness and tenderness in him, but he primarily feels mastery over her. Such qualities do not make Gabriel sympathetic, but rather make him an example of a man whose inner life struggles to keep pace with and adjust to the world around him. The Morkans' party exposes Gabriel as a social performer. He carefully reviews his thoughts and words, and he flounders in situations where he cannot predict another person's feelings. Gabriel's unease with unbridled feeling is palpable, but he must face his discomfort throughout the story. He illustrates the tense intersection of social isolation and personal confrontation.

Gabriel has one moment of spontaneous, honest speech, rare in "The Dead" as well as in *Dubliners* as a whole. When he dances with Miss Ivors, she interrogates him about his plans to travel in countries other than Ireland and asks him why he won't stay in Ireland and learn more about his own country. Instead of replying with niceties, Gabriel responds, "I'm sick of my own country, sick of it!" He is the sole character in *Dubliners* to voice his unhappiness with life in Ireland. While each story implicitly or explicitly connects the characters' hardships to Dublin, Gabriel pronounces his sentiment clearly and without remorse. This purgative exclamation highlights the symbolism of Gabriel's name, which he shares with the angel who informed Mary that she would be the mother of Christ in biblical history. Gabriel delivers his own message not only to Miss Ivors but also to himself and to the readers of "The Dead." He is the unusual character in *Dubliners* who dwells on his own revelation without suppressing or rejecting it, and who can place himself in a greater perspective. In the final scene of the story, when he intensely contemplates the meaning of his life, Gabriel has a vision not only of his own tedious life but of his role as a human.

EVELINE, "EVELINE"

Torn between two extreme options—unhappy domesticity or a dramatic escape to Argentina for marriage—Eveline has no possibility of a moderately content life. Her dilemma does not illustrate indecisiveness but rather the lack of options for someone in her position. On the docks, when she must make a choice once and for all, Eveline remembers her promise to her mother to keep the family together. So close to escape, Eveline revises her view of her life at home, remembering the small kindnesses: her father's caring for her when she was sick, a family picnic before her mother died. These memories overshadow the reality of her abusive father and deadening job, and her sudden certainty comes as an epiphany—she must remain with what is familiar. When faced with the clear choice between happiness and unhappiness, Eveline chooses unhappiness, which frightens her less than her intense emotions for Frank. Eveline's nagging sense of family duty stems from her fear of love and an unknown life abroad, and her decision to stay in Dublin renders her as just another figure in the crowd of Dubliners watching lovers and friends depart the city.

Eveline holds an important place in the overall narrative of *Dubliners*. Her story is the first in the collection that uses third-person narration, the first in the collection to focus on a female protagonist, and the only one in the collection that takes a character's name as the title. Eveline is also the first central adult character. For all of these reasons, she marks a crucial transition in the collection: Eveline in many ways is just another Dubliner, but she also broadens the perspective of *Dubliners*. Her story, rather than being limited by the first-person narration of earlier stories, suggests something about the hardships and limitations of women in early twentieth-century Dublin in general. Eveline's tortured decision about her life also sets a tone of restraint and fear that resonates in many of the later stories. Other female characters in *Dubliners* explore different harsh conditions of life in Dublin, but Eveline, in facing and rejecting a life-altering decision, remains the most tragic.

FARRINGTON, "COUNTERPARTS"

One of the darkest characters in *Dubliners*, Farrington rebels violently against his dull, routine life. He experiences paralyzing, mechanical repetition day after day as a copy clerk, and his mind-numbing tasks and uncompromising boss cause rage to simmer inside him. After the day in question in "Counterparts," the rage becomes so explosive that Farrington unleashes it on the most innocent figure in his world, one of his children. The root of Farrington's problem is his inability to realize the maddening circularity that defines his days. Farrington has no boundaries between the different parts of his world: his work life mimics his social life and his family life. No one part of his life can serve as an escape from any other part because each element has the potential to enrage him. Farrington consistently makes life worse for himself, not better. He slips away from work as he pleases, insults his boss, and matter-of-factly pawns his watch to buy alcohol. Though each small rebellion makes him momentarily happy, the displaced rage simply reappears someplace else, usually exacerbated by his actions. This lack of mindfulness about the consequences of his actions spills over into Farrington's anger, over which he appears to have little or no control.

Farrington's explosive violence sets him apart from some of the other characters in *Dubliners*, who often accept routine and boredom as facts of life and do little to upset the balance of familiarity and calm they've established. Mr. Duffy in "A Painful Case," for example, identifies so fully with his routines that he cannot upset them even for the chance of love. Eveline, too, chooses her familiar routines instead of leaping into the unknown, even though those routines are far inferior to the possibilities before her. Farrington's insensitivity to the people around him also casts him as the opposite of Eveline, whose concern for what others will think of her overrides her own desires. As the brutal bully of *Dubliners*, Farrington shows what can happen when a life consists primarily of mindless repetition: sooner or later violence will surface, and those who witness or are subject to the violence may themselves act violently in the future.

"ARABY" NARRATOR

The "Araby" narrator's experience of love moves him from placid youth to elation to frustrated loneliness as he explores the threshold between childhood and adulthood. Like the narrator of "An Encounter," he yearns to experience new places and things, but he is also like Eveline and other adult characters who grapple with the conflict between everyday life and the promise of love. He wants to see himself as an adult, so he dismisses his distracting schoolwork as "child's play" and expresses his intense emotions in dramatic, romantic gestures. However, his inability to actively pursue what he desires traps him in a child's world. His dilemma suggests the hope of youth stymied by the unavoidable realities of Dublin life. The "Araby" narrator is the last of the first-person narrators in *Dubliners*, all of whom are young boys.

CHARACTER ANALYSIS

THEMES, MOTIFS, AND SYMBOLS

THEMES

Themes are the fundamental and often universal ideas explored in a literary work.

THE PRISON OF ROUTINE

Restrictive routines and the repetitive, mundane details of everyday life mark the lives of Joyce's Dubliners and trap them in circles of frustration, restraint, and violence. Routine affects characters who face difficult predicaments, but it also affects characters who have little open conflict in their lives. The young boy of "An Encounter" yearns for a respite from the rather innocent routine of school, only to find himself sitting in a field listening to a man recycle disturbing thoughts. In "Counterparts," Farrington, who makes a living copying documents, demonstrates the dangerous potential of repetition. Farrington's work mirrors his social and home life, causing his anger—and abusive behavior—to worsen. Farrington, with his explosive physical reactions, illustrates more than any other character the brutal ramifications of a repetitive existence.

The most consistent consequences of following mundane routines are loneliness and unrequited love. In "Araby," a young boy wants to go to the bazaar to buy a gift for the girl he loves, but he is late because his uncle becomes mired in the routine of his workday. In "A Painful Case" Mr. Duffy's obsession with his predictable life costs him a golden chance at love. Eveline, in the story that shares her name, gives up her chance at love by choosing her familiar life over an unknown adventure, even though her familiar routines are tinged with sadness and abuse. The circularity of these Dubliners' lives effectively traps them, preventing them from being receptive to new experiences and happiness.

THE DESIRE FOR ESCAPE

The characters in *Dubliners* may be citizens of the Irish capital, but many of them long for escape and adventure in other countries. Such longings, however, are never actually realized by the stories' protagonists. The schoolboy yearning for escape and Wild West excitement in "An Encounter" is relegated to the imagination and to the confines of Dublin, while Eveline's hopes for a new life in Argentina dissolve on the docks of the city's river. Little Chandler enviously fantasizes about the London press job of his old friend and his travels to liberal cities like Paris, but the shame he feels about such desires stops him from taking action to pursue similar goals. More often than offering a literal escape from a physical place, the stories tell of opportunities to escape from smaller, more personal restraints. Eveline, for example, seeks release from domestic duties through marriage. In "Two Gallants," Lenehan wishes to escape his life of schemes, but he cannot take action to do so. Mr. Doran wishes to escape marrying Polly in "A Boarding House," but he knows he must relent. The impulse to escape from unhappy situations defines Joyce's Dubliners, as does the inability to actually undertake the process.

The Intersection of Life and Death

Dubliners opens with "The Sisters," which explores death and the process of remembering the dead, and closes with "The Dead," which invokes the quiet calm of snow that covers both the dead and the living. These stories bookend the collection and emphasize its consistent focus on the meeting point between life and death. Encounters between the newly dead and the living, such as in "The Sisters" and "A Painful Case," explicitly explore this meeting point, showing what kind of aftershocks a death can have for the living. Mr. Duffy, for example, reevaluates his life after learning about Mrs. Sinico's death in "A Painful Case," while the narrator of "The Sisters" doesn't know what to feel upon the death of the priest. In other stories, including "Eveline," "Ivy Day in the Committee Room," and "The Dead," memories of the dead haunt the living and color every action. In "Ivy Day," for example, Parnell hovers in the political talk.

The dead cast a shadow on the present, drawing attention to the mistakes and failures that people make generation after generation. Such overlap underscores Joyce's interest in life cycles and their repetition, and also his concern about those "living dead" figures like Maria in "Clay" who move through life with little excitement or emotion except in reaction to everyday snags and delays. The monotony of Dublin life leads Dubliners to live in a suspended state between life and death, in which each person has a pulse but is incapable of profound, life-sustaining action.

MOTIFS

Motifs are recurring structures, contrasts, or literary devices that can help to develop and inform the text's major themes.

PARALYSIS

In most of the stories in *Dubliners*, a character has a desire, faces obstacles to it, then ultimately relents and suddenly stops all action. These moments of paralysis show the characters' inability to change their lives and reverse the routines that hamper their wishes. Such immobility fixes the Dubliners in cycles of experience. The young boy in "Araby" halts in the middle of the dark bazaar, knowing that he will never escape the tedious delays of Dublin and attain love. Eveline freezes like an animal, fearing the possible new experience of life away from home. These moments evoke the theme of death in life as they show characters in a state of inaction and numbness. The opening story introduces this motif through the character of Father Flynn, whose literal paralysis traps him in a state suspended between life and death. Throughout the collection, this stifling state appears as part of daily life in Dublin, which all Dubliners ultimately acknowledge and accept.

EPIPHANY

Characters in *Dubliners* experience both great and small revelations in their everyday lives, moments that Joyce himself referred to as "epiphanies," a word with connotations of religious revelation. These epiphanies do not bring new experiences and the possibility of reform, as one might expect such moments to. Rather, these epiphanies allow characters to better understand their particular circumstances, usually rife with sadness and routine, which they then return to with resignation and frustration. Sometimes epiphanies occur only on the narrative level, serving as signposts to the reader that a story's character has missed a moment of self-reflection. For example, in "Clay," during the Halloween game when Maria touches the clay, which signifies an early death, she thinks nothing of it, overlooking a moment that could have revealed something about herself or the people around her. "Araby," "Eveline," "A Little Cloud," "A Painful Case," and "The Dead" all conclude with epiphanies that the characters fully register, yet these epiphanies are tinged with frustration, sadness, and regret. At the end of "The Dead," Gabriel's revelation clarifies the connection between the dead and the living, an epiphany that resonates throughout *Dubliners* as a whole. The epiphany motif highlights the repeated routine of hope and passive acceptance that marks each of these portraits, as well as the general human condition.

BETRAYAL

Deception, deceit, and treachery scar nearly every relationship in the stories in *Dubliners*, demonstrating the unease with which people attempt to connect with each other, both platonically and romantically. In "The Boarding House," Mrs. Mooney traps Mr. Doran into marrying her daughter Polly, and Mr. Doran dreads the union but will meet his obligation to pursue it. In "Two Gallants," Lenehan and Corley both suspect each other of cheating and scheming, though they join forces to swindle innocent housemaids out of their livelihoods. Concerns about betrayal frame the conversations in "Ivy Day in the Committee Room," particularly as Parnell's supporters see his demise as the result of pro-British treachery. Until his affair was exposed, Parnell had been a popular and influential politician, and many Irish believe the British were responsible for his downfall. All of the men in "Ivy Day" display wavering beliefs that suggest betrayal looms in Ireland's political present. In "The Dead," Gabriel feels betrayed by his wife's emotional outpouring for a former lover. This feeling evokes not only the sense of displacement and humiliation that all of these Dubliners fear but also the tendency for people to categorize many acts as "betrayal" in order to shift blame from themselves onto others.

RELIGION

References to priests, religious belief, and spiritual experience appear throughout the stories in *Dubliners* and ultimately paint an unflattering portrait of religion. In the first story, "The Sisters," Father Flynn cannot keep a strong grip on the chalice and goes mad in a confessional box. This story marks religion's first appearance as a haunting but incompetent and dangerous component of Dublin life. The strange man of "An Encounter" wears the same clothing as Father Flynn, connecting his lascivious behavior, however remotely, to the Catholic Church. In "Grace," Father Purdon shares his name with Dublin's red-light district, one of many subtle ironies in that story. In "Grace," Tom Kernan's fall and absent redemption highlight the pretension and inefficacy of religion—religion is just another daily ritual of repetition that advances no one. In other stories, such as "Araby," religion acts as a metaphor for dedication that dwindles. The presence of so many religious references also suggests that religion traps Dubliners into thinking about their lives after death.

SYMBOLS

Symbols are objects, characters, figures, or colors used to represent abstract ideas or concepts.

WINDOWS

Windows in *Dubliners* consistently evoke the anticipation of events or encounters that are about to happen. For example, the narrator in "The Sisters" looks into a window each night, waiting for signs of Father Flynn's death, and the narrator in "Araby" watches from his parlor window for the appearance of Mangan's sister. The suspense for these young boys centers in that space separating the interior life from the exterior life. Windows also mark the threshold between domestic space and the outside world, and through them the characters in *Dubliners* observe their own lives as well as the lives of others. Both Eveline and Gabriel turn to windows when they reflect on their own situations, both of which center on the relationship between the individual and the individual's place in a larger context.

DUSK AND NIGHTTIME

Joyce's Dublin is perpetually dark. No streams of sunlight or cheery landscapes illuminate these stories. Instead, a spectrum of grey and black underscores their somber tone. Characters walk through Dublin at dusk, an in-between time that hovers between the activity of day and the stillness of night, and live their most profound moments in the darkness of late hours. These dark backdrops evoke the half-life or in-between state the characters in *Dubliners* occupy, both physically and emotionally, suggesting the intermingling of life and death that marks every story. In this state, life can exist and proceed, but the darkness renders Dubliners' experiences dire and doomed.

FOOD

Nearly all of the characters in *Dubliners* eat or drink, and in most cases food serves as a reminder of both the threatening dullness of routine and the joys and difficulties of togetherness. In "A Painful Case," Mr. Duffy's solitary, duplicated meals are finally interrupted by the shocking newspaper article that reports Mrs. Sinico's death. This interruption makes him realize that his habits isolate him from the love and happiness of "life's feast." The party meal in "The

Dead" might evoke conviviality, but the rigid order of the rich table instead suggests military battle. In "Two Gallants," Lenehan's quiet meal of peas and ginger beer allows him to dwell on his self-absorbed life, so lacking in meaningful relationships and security, while the constant imbibing in "After the Race" fuels Jimmy's attempts to convince himself he belongs with his upper-class companions. Food in *Dubliners* allows Joyce to portray his characters and their experiences through a substance that both sustains life yet also symbolizes its restraints.

Summary and Analysis

"The Sisters"

Summary

A young boy reflects on the impending death of his friend Father Flynn. Knowing that after three strokes the paralyzed priest has little time left, the boy makes a habit of walking past Father Flynn's house, looking for the light of the traditional two candles placed on a coffin that would indicate his death. Each time, the boy thinks of the word *paralysis*. One night at his aunt and uncle's house, the boy arrives at supper to find his uncle and Old Cotter, a family friend, sitting before the fire. Old Cotter has come to the house to share the news that Father Flynn is dead. Knowing that everyone waits for his reaction, the boy remains quiet.

While the aunt shuffles food to and from the table, a conversation ensues between the uncle and Old Cotter, and the uncle notes the high hopes Father Flynn had for the boy. He hints that Father Flynn planned to prepare the boy for the priesthood and remarks on the friendship between them. Old Cotter, however, thinks of Father Flynn as a "peculiar case" and insists that young boys should play with people their own age. While the uncle agrees with Old Cotter, the aunt is disturbed that anyone could think critically of Father Flynn. She asks Old Cotter to clarify his point, but Old Cotter trails off and the conversation ends. That night, Old Cotter's comments keep the boy awake, and he dreams of Father Flynn smiling and confessing something to him.

The next morning the boy visits Father Flynn's house, where a bouquet of flowers and a card hang from the door handle. Instead of knocking, he walks away and reminisces about the time he spent there. He used to bring Father Flynn snuffing tobacco from his aunt, and Father Flynn would teach him things, such as Latin pronunciation and the parts of the Mass. Remembering Old Cotter's cryptic comments, the boy then tries to recall more of his dream from the night before, but he can remember only a Persian setting—he cannot remember the end. That evening the boy visits the house with his aunt, and they kneel at Father Flynn's open coffin with one of Father Flynn's sisters, Nannie, to pray. Afterward, the three retire to another room to join Eliza, Father Flynn's other sister. Over sherry and crackers they discuss Father Flynn's death, his taxing career as a priest, and the helpful services of Father O'Rourke, another priest who anointed Father Flynn and completed all of the necessary paperwork and death notices. All the while the boy remains quiet. The story ends with Eliza's recollection of Father Flynn's increasingly odd behavior, which started with dropping a chalice during Mass. When one night Father O'Rourke and another priest found Father Flynn shut in a confessional box, laughing to himself, they finally realized he was sick.

ANALYSIS

In "The Sisters," and in the rest of the stories in *Dubliners*, strange and puzzling events occur that remain unexplained. Father Flynn suffers from paralyzing strokes and eventually dies, but his deterioration, epitomized by his laughing frenzy in a confessional box, also hints that he was mentally unstable. The reader never learns exactly what was wrong with him. Similarly, Father Flynn and the young narrator had a relationship that Old Cotter thinks was unhealthy, but that the narrator paints as spiritual when he recounts the discussions he and Father Flynn had about Church rituals. However, the narrator also has strange dreams about Father Flynn and admits to feeling uncomfortable around him. Joyce presents just enough information so that the reader suspects Father Flynn is a malevolent figure, but never enough so that the reader knows the full story. Such a technique is hinted at in the first paragraph of the story. The narrator thinks of the word *paralysis* when looking at Father Flynn's window and says the word sounds strange, like the word *gnomon*, a term that generally refers to instruments, like the hand on a sundial, that indicate something. Joyce does exactly that: He points to details and suggestions, but never completes the puzzle.

The physical presence of Father Flynn lingers throughout the story, coloring the narrator's experience of dealing with death in life and showing how a death interrupts normal human activities. Father Flynn plays a fleshly role in the story. His approaching death makes the narrator think of the corpse, which he eventually sees. When Father Flynn dies, the narrator continues to think of his physical presence, particularly the lurid way in which his tongue rested on his lip, and dreams of his face. Such bizarre physical images evoke the awkward nature of death. Like the episodes of Father Flynn's odd behavior that the sisters recount, the narrator's memories give Father Flynn a haunting presence that is fearful and mysterious, not beautiful and neat. In the final scene with the sisters, eating, drinking, and talking become difficult since death frames those activities. After viewing the corpse, the narrator declines the crackers offered because he fears that eating them would make too much noise, as if he might disturb Father Flynn in his coffin. Similarly, the narrator's aunt is unable to broach the subject of death. She asks questions about how Father Flynn died, but her thoughts trail off. Father Flynn may be dead, but in many ways he is still very present among the living.

The inability of the narrator and his aunt to eat and speak during their visit to the sisters recalls the sense of paralysis that the narrator connects to the dying Father Flynn in the story's opening paragraph. This link between paralysis or inaction to both death and religion underpins all the stories in *Dubliners*. Characters face events that paralyze them from taking action or fulfilling their desires, as though they experience a kind of death in life. In "The Sisters," such paralysis is connected to religion through Father Flynn. Father Flynn's dropping of the chalice and his inability to grasp the same object in his coffin suggest that the rituals of religion lead to paralysis. His sisters also attribute his demise to the strains of clerical life. The crippling quality of religion resurfaces in other stories like "Grace," in which Joyce more directly questions the role of the Church in the lives of Dubliners.

This story opens with an image of a Dubliner gazing through a window and reflecting on a dilemma. Such a symbol appears throughout the collection, and here it is particularly important because it draws attention to the narrative point of view. "The Sisters" is the first of three stories in the collection told in first-person point of view. As in the other two stories, "An Encounter" and "Araby," the narrator never divulges his name and rarely participates in the conversations. The opening image of the window in the first paragraph reinforces this sense of quiet, detached observation, which the narrators of the later stories adopt. Through this narrative technique Joyce suggests that even first-hand experience is in some ways voyeuristic, and that it's possible for a person to observe his or her own life from the outside.

"An Encounter"

Summary
Imagining they are in the Wild West, a group of schoolboys stage mock "cowboy and Indian" battles. The narrator, an unnamed boy, explains that Joe Dillon, the host and consistent winner, always ends his victory with a dance. Such games and the fictional adventure stories on which they are based bond these boys together, both in leisurely release and secrecy. As the narrator explains, he and his fellow students surreptitiously circulate the magazines that carry the stories at school. The narrator recalls one time when Father Butler caught Leo Dillon, Joe's younger brother, with one such publication in his pocket. Father Butler scolded Leo for reading such material instead of his Roman history.

The narrator yearns for more concrete adventures and organizes a plan with Leo and another boy named Mahony to skip school one day and walk through Dublin, visiting the ships along the wharf and finally the Pigeon House, Dublin's electrical power station. He confirms the pact by collecting sixpence from Leo and Mahony, and they all promise to meet at ten the next morning. However, only Mahony arrives as agreed. While the narrator and Mahony walk south through North Dublin, two poor boys approach them and yell insults, thinking them Protestant. Resisting retribution, the boys continue until they reach the river, and there they buy some food and watch the Dublin water traffic and laborers. They cross the river in a ferryboat, buy some more food on the other side, and wander the streets until they reach an open field where they rest on a slope.

The boys are alone for a while until an older man appears in the distance, walking toward them leaning on a stick. He gradually approaches and passes the boys, but then backtracks and joins them. The man begins to talk, reminiscing about his boyhood and talking about books, such as the works of Lord Lytton, who wrote romances. The conversation then turns to "sweethearts" as the man asks the boys if they have many girlfriends, a question that surprises the narrator. As the story continues, the narrator notes the peculiar appearance and behavior of the man: his yellow-toothed, gaped smile, how he twitched occasionally, and, most of all, his monotonous repetition of phrases.

When the man leaves for a moment, the narrator suggests that he and Mahony assume the code names of Smith and Murphy, to be safe. As the man returns, Mahony runs off to chase a stray cat, leaving the narrator to listen to the man's peculiar monologues alone. The man remarks that Mahony seems like the kind of boy that gets whipped at school, and from there launches into a diatribe about disciplining boys who misbehave, insisting that any boy who talks to a girl should be whipped, and that he himself would enjoy executing the punishment. At a pause in the man's speech, the narrator rises and announces that he must depart. He calls for Mahony, using the name Murphy, who runs across the field toward him in response.

ANALYSIS

"An Encounter" suggests that although people yearn for escape and adventure, routine is inevitable, and new experiences, when they do come, can be profoundly disturbing. The narrator and his friends play games about the Wild West to disrupt the rote activity of school, and venture into Dublin for the same reason. However, the narrator and his friends never fully reach escape. Though the narrator bemoans the restraint of school, his attempt to avoid it leads him to the discomforting encounter with an old man whose fixation on erotic novels, girlfriends, and whipping casts him as a pervert. This creepy figure serves as an embodiment of routine and suggests that repetition exists even within strange new experiences. The man walks in circles, approaching and passing the boys before retracing his steps to join them. He mimics this action in his speech by repeating points already raised and lingering on topics uncomfortable for the narrator. Although these boys seek an escape, they must suffer monotony, in the form of an excruciating afternoon with a frightening man. The rather mundane title for the story suggests that this deeply awkward and anxious meeting is not so atypical of Dublin life, nor of childhood.

The troubling presence of a strange older man recalls the ambiguous relationship between Father Flynn and the narrator of "The Sisters," but this story clearly shows the man exploiting and abusing the innocence of youth. The man's conversation becomes more and more inappropriate and threatening, culminating in his fantasy about whipping Mahony. Most dangerous, the circular manner of his speech paralyzes the narrator. The man's orbit of words both mesmerizes and disturbs him, and he can do nothing but stare at the ground and listen. When the man abruptly rises to walk away and, presumably, exposes himself to the boys, the narrator remains frozen like a startled victim. In this state, the narrator knows something is wrong, since he suggests to Mahony that they assume fake names, but he does not run away. Even when the man returns and Mahony runs away to chase a cat, the narrator stays rooted to the ground. Exactly why the narrator experiences this paralysis is not explained, but its effects are anything but neutral.

Many references to religion hover in "An Encounter," demonstrating that religion is a fixture in Dublin life that even the boys' imaginations cannot elude. When Father Butler chastises Leo about the magazine, he scolds that only Protestant boys, not Catholic boys like Leo, would read such fanciful stories. This insult introduces the tension between Catholics and Protestants that Joyce alludes to throughout *Dubliners*, and reveals it to be a routine fact of life in Ireland. Religious tension appears again when two poor boys throw rocks at the narrator and Mahony and mistake them for Protestants, an incident that suggests that the line between these staunchly opposed groups is blurry. The narrator, using words like *chivalry* and *siege*, pretends that he and Mahony are in a battle, but the playfulness of such imaginary games only reinforces the authenticity of the scene. Imagination can mask experiences, Joyce suggests, but it cannot reverse them or make them disappear.

"ARABY"

> *I watched my master's face pass from amiability to*
> *sternness; he hoped I was not beginning to idle. I could*
> *not call my wandering thoughts together. I had hardly*
> *any patience with the serious work of life which, now*
> *that it stood between me and my desire, seemed to me*
> *child's play, ugly monotonous child's play.*
>
> *(See* QUOTATIONS, *p. 68)*

SUMMARY

The narrator, an unnamed boy, describes the North Dublin street on which his house is located. He thinks about the priest who died in the house before his family moved in and the games that he and his friends played in the street. He recalls how they would run through the back lanes of the houses and hide in the shadows when they reached the street again, hoping to avoid people in the neighborhood, particularly the boy's uncle or the sister of his friend Mangan. The sister often comes to the front of their house to call the brother, a moment that the narrator savors.

Every day begins for this narrator with such glimpses of Mangan's sister. He places himself in the front room of his house so he can see her leave her house, and then he rushes out to walk behind her quietly until finally passing her. The narrator and Mangan's sister talk little, but she is always in his thoughts. He thinks about her when he accompanies his aunt to do food shopping on Saturday evening in the busy marketplace and when he sits in the back room of his house alone. The narrator's infatuation is so intense that he fears he will never gather the courage to speak with the girl and express his feelings.

One morning, Mangan's sister asks the narrator if he plans to go to Araby, a Dublin bazaar. She notes that she cannot attend, as she has already committed to attend a retreat with her school. Having recovered from the shock of the conversation, the narrator offers to bring her something from the bazaar. This brief meeting launches the narrator into a period of eager, restless waiting and fidgety tension in anticipation of the bazaar. He cannot focus in school. He finds the lessons tedious, and they distract him from thinking about Mangan's sister.

On the morning of the bazaar the narrator reminds his uncle that he plans to attend the event so that the uncle will return home early and provide train fare. Yet dinner passes and a guest visits, but the uncle does not return. The narrator impatiently endures the time passing, until at 9 P.M. the uncle finally returns, unbothered that he has forgotten about the narrator's plans. Reciting the epigram "All work and no play makes Jack a dull boy," the uncle gives the narrator the money and asks him if he knows the poem "The Arab's Farewell to his Steed." The narrator leaves just as his uncle begins to recite the lines, and, thanks to eternally slow trains, arrives at the bazaar just before 10 P.M., when it is starting to close down. He approaches one stall that is still open, but buys nothing, feeling unwanted by the woman watching over the goods. With no purchase for Mangan's sister, the narrator stands angrily in the deserted bazaar as the lights go out.

ANALYSIS

In "Araby," the allure of new love and distant places mingles with the familiarity of everyday drudgery, with frustrating consequences. Mangan's sister embodies this mingling, since she is part of the familiar surroundings of the narrator's street as well as the exotic promise of the bazaar. She is a "brown figure" who both reflects the brown façades of the buildings that line the street and evokes the skin color of romanticized images of Arabia that flood the narrator's head. Like the bazaar that offers experiences that differ from everyday Dublin, Mangan's sister intoxicates the narrator with new feelings of joy and elation. His love for her, however, must compete with the dullness of schoolwork, his uncle's lateness, and the Dublin trains. Though he promises Mangan's sister that he will go to Araby and purchase a gift for her, these mundane realities undermine his plans and ultimately thwart his desires. The narrator arrives at the bazaar only to encounter flowered teacups and English accents, not the freedom of the enchanting East. As the bazaar closes down, he realizes that Mangan's sister will fail his expectations as well, and that his desire for her is actually only a vain wish for change.

The narrator's change of heart concludes the story on a moment of epiphany, but not a positive one. Instead of reaffirming his love or realizing that he does not need gifts to express his feelings for Mangan's sister, the narrator simply gives up. He seems to interpret his arrival at the bazaar as it fades into darkness as a sign that his relationship with Mangan's sister will also remain just a wishful idea and that his infatuation was as misguided as his fantasies about the bazaar. What might have been a story of happy, youthful love becomes a tragic story of defeat. Much like the disturbing, unfulfilling adventure in "An Encounter," the narrator's failure at the bazaar suggests that fulfillment and contentedness remain foreign to Dubliners, even in the most unusual events of the city like an annual bazaar.

The tedious events that delay the narrator's trip indicate that no room exists for love in the daily lives of Dubliners, and the absence of love renders the characters in the story almost anonymous. Though the narrator might imagine himself to be carrying thoughts of Mangan's sister through his day as a priest would carry a Eucharistic chalice to an altar, the minutes tick away through school, dinner, and his uncle's boring poetic recitation. Time does not adhere to the narrator's visions of his relationship. The story presents this frustration as universal: the narrator is nameless, the girl is always "Mangan's sister" as though she is any girl next door, and the story closes with the narrator imagining himself as a creature. In "Araby," Joyce suggests that all people experience frustrated desire for love and new experiences.

"EVELINE"

SUMMARY

Eveline Hill sits at a window in her home and looks out onto the street while fondly recalling her childhood, when she played with other children in a field now developed with new homes. Her thoughts turn to her sometimes abusive father with whom she lives, and to the prospect of freeing herself from her hard life juggling jobs as a shop worker and a nanny to support herself and her father. Eveline faces a difficult dilemma: remain at home like a dutiful daughter, or leave Dublin with her lover, Frank, who is a sailor. He wants her to marry him and live with him in Buenos Aires, and she has already agreed to leave with him in secret. As Eveline recalls, Frank's courtship of her was pleasant until her father began to voice his disapproval and bicker with Frank. After that, the two lovers met clandestinely.

As Eveline reviews her decision to embark on a new life, she holds in her lap two letters, one to her father and one to her brother Harry. She begins to favor the sunnier memories of her old family life, when her mother was alive and her brother was living at home, and notes that she did promise her mother to dedicate herself to maintaining the home. She reasons that her life at home, cleaning and cooking, is hard but perhaps not the worst option—her father is not always mean, after all. The sound of a street organ then reminds her of her mother's death, and her thoughts change course. She remembers her mother's uneventful, sad life, and passionately embraces her decision to escape the same fate by leaving with Frank.

At the docks in Dublin, Eveline waits in a crowd to board the ship with Frank. She appears detached and worried, overwhelmed by the images around her, and prays to God for direction. Her previous declaration of intent seems to have never happened. When the boat whistle blows and Frank pulls on her hand to lead her with him, Eveline resists. She clutches the barrier as Frank is swept into the throng moving toward the ship. He continually shouts "Come!" but Eveline remains fixed to the land, motionless and emotionless.

ANALYSIS

Eveline's story illustrates the pitfalls of holding onto the past when facing the future. Hers is the first portrait of a female in *Dubliners*, and it reflects the conflicting pull many women in early twentieth-century Dublin felt between a domestic life rooted in the past and the possibility of a new married life abroad. One moment, Eveline feels happy to leave her hard life, yet at the next moment she worries about fulfilling promises to her dead mother. She grasps the letters she's written to her father and brother, revealing her inability to let go of those family relationships, despite her father's cruelty and her brother's absence. She clings to the older and more pleasant memories and imagines what other people want her to do or will do for her. She sees Frank as a rescuer, saving her from her domestic situation. Eveline suspends herself between the call of home and the past and the call of new experiences and the future, unable to make a decision.

The threat of repeating her mother's life spurs Eveline's epiphany that she must leave with Frank and embark on a new phase in her life, but this realization is short-lived. She hears a street organ, and when she remembers the street organ that played on the night before her mother's death, Eveline resolves not to repeat her mother's life of "commonplace sacrifices closing in final craziness," but she does exactly that. Like the young boys of "An Encounter" and "Araby," she desires escape, but her reliance on routine and repetition over-rides such impulses. On the docks with Frank, away from the famil-iarity of home, Eveline seeks guidance in the routine habit of prayer. Her action is the first sign that she in fact hasn't made a decision, but instead remains fixed in a circle of indecision. She will keep her lips moving in the safe practice of repetitive prayer rather than join her love on a new and different path. Though Eveline fears that Frank will drown her in their new life, her reliance on everyday rituals is what causes Eveline to freeze and not follow Frank onto the ship.

Eveline's paralysis within an orbit of repetition leaves her a "helpless animal," stripped of human will and emotion. The story does not suggest that Eveline placidly returns home and continues her life, but shows her transformation into an automaton that lacks expression. Eveline, the story suggests, will hover in mindless repe-tition, on her own, in Dublin. On the docks with Frank, the possi-bility of living a fully realized life left her.

"AFTER THE RACE"

SUMMARY

As many flashy cars drive toward Dublin, crowds gather and cheer. A race has just finished, and though the French have placed second and third after the German-Belgian team, the local sightseers loudly support them. Jimmy Doyle rides in one of the cars with his wealthy

French friend, Charles Ségouin, whom he met while studying at Cambridge. Two other men ride with them as well: Ségouin's Canadian cousin, André Riviére, and a Hungarian pianist, Villona. Driving back into Dublin, the young men rejoice about the victory, and Jimmy enjoys the prestige of the ride. He fondly thinks about his recent investment in Ségouin's motor-company business venture, a financial backing that his father, a successful butcher, approves and supports. Jimmy savors the notoriety of being surrounded by and seen with such glamorous company, and in such a luxurious car.

Ségouin drops Jimmy and Villona off in Dublin so they can return to Jimmy's home, where Villona is staying, to change into formal dress for dinner at Ségouin's hotel. Jimmy's proud parents dote on their smartly dressed and well-connected son. At the dinner, the reunited party joins an Englishman, Routh, and conversation energetically moves from music to cars to politics, under the direction of Ségouin. Jimmy, turning to Irish-English relations, rouses an angry response from Routh, but Ségouin expertly snuffs any potential for argument with a toast.

After the meal, the young men stroll through Dublin and run into another acquaintance, an American named Farley, who invites them to his yacht. The party grows merrier, and they sing a French marching song as they make their way to the harbor. Once on board, the men proceed to dance and drink as Villona plays the piano. Jimmy makes a speech that his companions loudly applaud, and then the men settle down to play cards. Drunk and giddy, Jimmy plays game after game, losing more and more money. He yearns for the playing to stop, but goes along nevertheless. A final game leaves Routh the champion. Even as the biggest loser alongside Farley, Jimmy's spirits never dwindle. He knows he will feel remorse the next day, but assures himself of his happiness just as Villona opens the cabin door and announces that daybreak has come.

ANALYSIS

"After the Race" explores the potentially destructive desire for money and status. The monetary standing and social connections of most of the characters are explored, but the story focuses on the efforts of Jimmy, and to some extent Jimmy's father, to fit into an affluent class. Jimmy is completely unburdened and childishly whimsical about life and money, as his father fosters Jimmy's lush lifestyle. Having earned a large income from wise contracts and retail developments in his butchery business, the father provides

Jimmy with a prestigious education at Cambridge, where he gains Ségouin's coveted friendship. However, this potentially sunny portrait of carefree wealth and prestige is dulled by the less impressive excesses of success. Jimmy's studies focus mainly on social outings and spending, and at the end of "After the Race" Jimmy emerges not as a dashing, popular bachelor, but as a clueless fool, his pockets empty after a spate of card games in which he was barely sober enough to participate. Indeed, Jimmy hardly seems cognizant of himself as a person, but highly aware of where and with whom he is seen. For Jimmy, seeking riches and notoriety leads only to poverty and embarrassment.

Like many of the characters in *Dubliners*, Jimmy has a moment of revelation in which he recognizes the truth of his situation, but he does nothing to change it. After he loses ruinously at cards, Jimmy hangs his head in his hands, knowing that regret will set in the next day. The irony of the conclusion is that the next day is already there, that daybreak has come. Jimmy, the story suggests, always faces the reality of his feigned wealth and his follies, but he also always avoids it. Regret lurks constantly beneath the surface of his actions, yet he continuously puts off fully acknowledging it. Jimmy instead submerses himself in his infatuation with signs of wealth. He relishes the experience of riding in the French car, exclaiming to himself how stylish the group must look. Such statements reveal Jimmy as intoxicated with presentation and committed to convincing himself of his rightful place in the group. When Jimmy delivers his speech on the yacht, he cannot remember what he says only moments after finishing, but assures himself that it must have been decent if such excellent people applauded him. The story casts Jimmy as simple and passive, placing trust in money that constantly eludes him.

"After the Race" highlights the political interests that underpin the Doyle family's clamoring for money. The father's profitable business that gives leisure to Jimmy flourished at the cost of his political views. Though once a fervent supporter of Irish independence, the father makes his money on contracts with the same police who uphold British law. He also acts against the national interests of promoting all things Irish by sending his son to England and encouraging his investments in French business ventures. When Jimmy attempts to talk about such popularly debated issues at the dinner table, his voice is silenced. The Englishman leaves this story the winner. Like the luxury cars that speed away from the countryside to return to the continent in the opening of the story, all money seems to flee from Jimmy's pockets into those of others by the end of the story. The Irish, "After the Race" implies, always finish in last place.

"TWO GALLANTS"

SUMMARY

Lenehan and Corley, two men whose occupations are suspiciously vague, walk through the streets of central Dublin after a day of drinking in a bar. Corley dominates the conversation, chatting about his latest romantic interest, a maid who works at a wealthy home and with whom he has a date that evening. He brags about the cigarettes and cigars the maid pilfers for him from the house and how he has expertly managed to avoid giving her his name. Lenehan listens patiently, occasionally offering a question or a clichéd response. As the men talk, they reveal a plan they've hatched to convince the maid to procure money from her employer's house. Lenehan repeatedly asks Corley if he thinks she is right for their business, which launches Corley into a short lecture on the utility of a good maid, or "slavey." Unlike other women who insist on being compensated, Corley explains, slaveys pitch in. He pauses wistfully to recall one of his former lovers who now works as a prostitute, and Lenehan teases that Corley, who seems to excel in pimping, must have encouraged such a profession.

The men resume discussing their plan, and Corley confirms that the maid will turn up as promised. They pass a harpist playing a mournful song about Irish legends, then approach the appointed corner where the maid is waiting. She is a young, ruddy-cheeked woman, dressed oddly with a sailor hat and tattered boa. Lenehan, impressed with Corley's taste, leers at her. Corley appears disgruntled, suspecting Lenehan of trying to squeeze him out of the plan. But as he leaves Lenehan to greet his date, he promises to walk past so Lenehan can look at her again. The men agree to meet later that night at a corner by the maid's house. Lenehan watches as Corley and the maid walk off, and he takes another intense look before positioning himself so he can watch the couple pass once more.

Finally alone, Lenehan aimlessly wanders through Dublin to pass the time. Not wishing to speak with anyone, Lenehan continues to walk until he stops into a bar for a quick meal of peas and ginger beer. Over his food, he sadly contemplates his life: instead of just scraping by, he wishes instead for a steady job and stable home life. Lenehan leaves the bar and, after running into some friends in the street, makes his way to meet Corley. Lenehan nervously smokes a cigarette, worrying that Corley has cut him out of the plan, before he spots Corley and the maid. He stealthily walks behind the couple until they stop at a posh residence, where the maid runs inside through the servant's entrance. In a moment, she emerges from the front door, meets Corley, and then runs back inside. Corley leaves. Lenehan runs after him, but Corley ignores his calls. Eventually, Corley stops and shows Lenehan a gold coin, a sign that the plan was successful.

<hr />

Analysis

The title of this story, "Two Gallants," is ironic because Corley and Lenehan are anything but fine, chivalrous men. Instead, they make an unpleasant practice of duping maids into stealing from their employers. Of the two men, Lenehan is the more self-reflective, and he provides a quiet, contemplative balance for the burly actions of Corley, who has crafted and executed their current plan. Lenehan is a Dublin man quite literally on the edge. He has one foot on the path and one on the road as he walks with Corley, he must bide time while Corley woos the girl, he lives on the verge of bankruptcy, and many consider him to be "a leech." At the age of thirty-one, Lenehan yearns for a comfortable life, but he is no less guilty of deceit than Corley is. Both men lead dissolute lives and have few prospects, and nothing but easy money gives them hope. The meanderings of the story ultimately lead to the gold coin, suggesting that for both of these men, the coin is their ultimate reward and desire.

Even though Lenehan and Corley use betrayal to make money, both men are anxious about treachery. Corley orchestrates his encounter with the maid defensively, allowing Lenehan only distant glimpses of the maid for fear of competition. Similarly, Lenehan pesters Corley about his choice of victim, worried that the plan will fall flat and leave him penniless yet again. When Corley and the maid reappear later than Lenehan expected, Lenehan momentarily convinces himself that Corley has cheated him out of the profits, and not until the final sentence of the story can we be certain that the men's collaboration is intact. This constant worry about betrayal reappears throughout *Dubliners* and always recalls Ireland's political scandal in which the politician Parnell, according to his loyal followers, was abandoned by the Irish government and many voters when news of his affair leaked into the press. Lenehan and Corley are part of a gen-

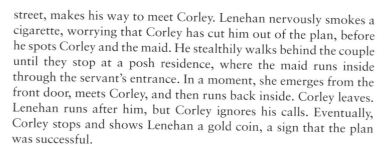

eration disappointed after Parnell's downfall who now feel they have no one to trust. This state of mind leads only to further betrayal.

Traditional national images connect Lenehan's and Corley's desperate and shallow lives with Ireland itself. For example, the harp, a traditional symbol of Ireland, appears in "Two Gallants." Outside a wealthy Anglo-Protestant gentleman's club, the men pass a harpist who is playing on a feminized, bare, and "weary" instrument. The harpist's melodies later follow Lenehan and pace his steps. While Corley gallivants with his maid, Lenehan acts as the harpist, tapping his hands to the notes as he walks through Dublin. This parallel suggests that Lenehan is in some ways guilty of the same swindling as Corley, of taking advantage of a "woman" in the form of his country. This ambiguous connection between Lenehan and the harp is typical of Joyce's national references. Joyce both leaves the inferences open to his readers and continually complicates them. When Lenehan later enjoys the meager feast of peas and ginger beer and reflects on his directionless life, for example, his meal reflects the colors of the Irish flag (the green peas and the orange ginger beer). Such associations link the maligned life to an image of the country, but with no conclusive sense of cause and effect, and no potential for solution.

"THE BOARDING HOUSE"

SUMMARY
After a difficult marriage with a drunken husband that ends in separation, Mrs. Mooney opens a boarding house to make a living. Her son, Jack, and daughter, Polly, live with her in the house, which is filled with clerks from the city, as well as occasional tourists and musicians. Mrs. Mooney runs a strict and tight business and is known by the lodgers as "The Madam." Polly, who used to work in an office, now stays at home at her mother's request, to amuse the lodgers and help with the cleaning. Surrounded by so many young men, Polly inevitably develops a relationship with one of them, Mr. Doran. Mrs. Mooney knows about the relationship, but instead of sending Polly back to work in the city, she monitors its developments. Polly becomes increasingly uncomfortable with her mother's lack of intervention, but Mrs. Mooney waits until "the right moment" to intercede. First she speaks awkwardly with Polly, then arranges to speak with Mr. Doran on a Sunday morning.

Mrs. Mooney looks forward to her confrontation, which she intends to "win" by defending her daughter's honor and convincing

Mr. Doran to offer his hand in marriage. Waiting for the time to pass, Mrs. Mooney figures the odds are in her favor, considering that Mr. Doran, who has worked for a wine merchant for thirteen years and garnered much respect, will choose the option that least harms his career.

Meanwhile, Mr. Doran anguishes over the impending meeting with Mrs. Mooney. As he clumsily grooms himself for the appointment, he reviews the difficult confession to his priest that he made on Saturday evening, in which he was harshly reproved for his romantic affair. He knows he can either marry Polly or run away, the latter an option that would ruin his sound reputation. Convincing himself that he has been duped, Mr. Doran bemoans Polly's unimpressive family, her ill manners, and her poor grammar, and wonders how he can remain free and unmarried. In this vexed moment Polly enters the room and threatens to end her life out of unhappiness. In her presence, Mr. Doran begins to remember how he was bewitched by Polly's beauty and kindness, but he still wavers about his decision.

Uneasy, Mr. Doran comforts Polly and departs for the meeting, leaving her to wait in the room. She rests on the bed crying for a while, neatens her appearance, and then nestles back in the bed, dreaming of her possible future with Mr. Doran. Finally, Mrs. Mooney interrupts the reverie by calling to her daughter. Mr. Doran, according to Mrs. Mooney, wants to speak with Polly.

ANALYSIS

In "The Boarding House," marriage offers promise and profit on the one hand, and entrapment and loss on the other. What begins as a simple affair becomes a tactical game of obligation and reparation. Mrs. Mooney's and Mr. Doran's propositions and hesitations suggest that marriage is more about social standards, public perception, and formal sanctions than about mere feelings. The character of Mrs. Mooney illustrates the challenges that a single mother of a daughter faces, but her scheme to marry Polly into a higher class mitigates any sympathetic response from the reader. Mrs. Mooney may have endured a difficult marriage and separation, but she now carries the dubious title of "The Madam," a term suggestive of her scrupulous managing of the house, but also of the head of whorehouse. Mrs. Mooney does, in fact, prostitute her daughter to some degree. She insists that Polly leave her office job and stay at home at the boarding house, in part so she might entertain, however innocently, the male lodgers. When a relationship blossoms, Mrs. Mooney tracks it until the most profitable moment—until she is sure Mr. Doran, a successful clerk, must propose to Polly out of social propriety. Mrs. Mooney justly insists that men should carry the same responsibility as women in these casual love affairs, but at the same time prides herself on her ability to rid herself of a dependent daughter so easily.

Mr. Doran agonizes about the limitations and loss of respect that marrying beneath him will bring, but he ultimately relents out of fear of social critique from his priest, his employer, Mrs. Mooney, and Polly's violent brother. When Polly visits him in distress he feels as helpless as she does, even though he tells her not to worry. He goes through the motions of what society expects of him, not according to what he intuitively feels. When he descends the stairs to meet with Mrs. Mooney, he yearns to escape but knows no one is on his side. The "force" that pushes him down the stairs is a force of anxiety about what others will think of him. While Mr. Doran's victimization by Mrs. Mooney evokes pity, his self-concern and harsh complaints about Polly's unpolished background and manner of speaking make him an equal counterpart to Mrs. Mooney. He worries little about Polly's integrity or feelings, and instead considers his years of hard work and good reputation now verging on destruction.

As a place where "everyone knows everyone else's business," the boarding house serves as a microcosm of Dublin. Various classes mix under its roof, but relationships are gauged and watched, class lines are constantly negotiated, and social standing must override emotions like love. The inhabitants are not free to do what they choose because unstated rules of decorum govern life in the house, just as they do in the city. Such rules maintain order, but they also ensnare people in awkward situations when they have competing and secret interests. Even the seemingly innocent Polly ultimately appears complicit in Mrs. Mooney's plot. After threatening to kill herself in despair, she suddenly appears happy and unbothered about the dilemma when she is left alone, and she knows Mr. Doran will comply with Mrs. Mooney's wishes. In "The Boarding House," marriage serves as a fixture of life that Dubliners cannot avoid, and the story shows that strategy and acceptance are the only means of survival.

"A Little Cloud"

He remembered the books of poetry upon his shelves at home. He had bought them in his bachelor days and many an evening, as he sat in the little room of the hall, he had been tempted to take one down from the bookshelf and read out something to his wife. But shyness always held him back; and so the books had remained on their shelves.

(See Quotations, *p. 69)*

Summary

Little Chandler eagerly awaits a reunion with his old friend Ignatius Gallaher, who moved to London eight years ago. A married man and father who earned his nickname from his small and delicate deportment, Little Chandler whittles away the afternoon hours at his clerical job, constantly thinking about his approaching evening drink. Little Chandler wonders in amazement at Gallaher's impressive career writing for English newspapers, though he never doubted that Gallaher would do well for himself. As Little Chandler leaves work and walks to the bar where the men agreed to meet, he contemplates Gallaher's homecoming and success, then thinks of his own stunted writing aspirations and the possibilities of life abroad that remain out of his reach. Little Chandler used to love poetry, but he gave it up when he got married. As he walks he considers the far-fetched possibility of writing his own book of poems.

In the bar, Little Chandler and Gallaher talk about foreign cities, marriage, and the future. Little Chandler is surprised to see Gallaher's unhealthy pallor and thinning hair, which Gallaher blames on the stress of press life. Throughout the conversation, during which the men consume three glasses of whiskey and smoke two cigars, Little Chandler simultaneously recoils from and admires Gallaher's gruff manners and tales of foreign cities. He is displeased with Gallaher's presumptuous way of addressing others and wonders about the immorality of a place like Paris with its infamous dance halls. At the same time, he envies Gallaher's worldliness and experience. Little Chandler has settled down with a wife and has a son. When he himself becomes the subject of conversation, he is uneasy and blushes. He manages to invite Gallaher to visit his home and meet his family that evening, but Gallaher explains that he has another appointment and must leave the bar soon. The men have their final drink together, and the conversation returns to and ends with Galla-her and his bachelorhood. When Little Chandler insists that Gallaher will one day marry, the journalist scoffs at the prospect, claiming that if he does so he will marry rich, but as it stands he is content to please himself with many women rather than become bored with one.

Later that night in his house, Little Chandler waits for his wife to come home from the local store—Chandler had forgotten to bring home coffee in his flurry of excitement about Gallaher. While he holds his baby son in his arms, as directed by his wife, he gazes at a picture of her and recounts his conversation with Gallaher. Unlike Gallaher's exotic, passionate mistresses, his wife appears cold and unfeeling, though pretty. Chandler begins to question his marriage and its trappings: a "little" house, a crying child. Reading a passage of Byron stirs his longings to write, but soon his wife returns home to snatch the screaming child from his arms and scold her husband. Little Chandler feels remorse for his rebellious thoughts.

ANALYSIS

"A Little Cloud" maps the frustrated aspirations Little Chandler has to change his life and pursue his dream of writing poetry. The story contrasts Little Chandler's dissatisfaction and temerity with Gallaher's bold writing career abroad. Little Chandler believes that to succeed in life, one must leave Dublin like Gallaher did. However, Gallaher's success is not altogether confirmed in this story, unless one measures his success by his straightforward, unrestrained take on life. Little Chandler compares himself to Gallaher, and in doing so blames his shortcomings on the restraints around him, such as Dublin, his wife, and his child. He hides from the truth that his aspirations to write are fanciful and shallow. Not once in the story does Little Chandler write, but he spends plenty of time imagining fame and indulging in poetic sentiments. He has a collection of poetry books but cannot muster the courage to read them aloud to his wife, instead remaining introverted and repeating lines to himself. He constantly thinks about his possible career as a poet of the Celtic school and envisions himself lauded by English critics, often to the extent that he mythologizes himself. Little Chandler uses his country to dream of success, but at the same time blames it for limiting that success.

While dreaming of a poetic career may provide escape for Little Chandler, the demands of work and home that serve as obstacles to his dreams ultimately overwhelm him. Like other characters in *Dubliners*, Little Chandler experiences an epiphany that makes him realize he will never change his life. Looking at a picture of his wife after returning home from the pub, Little Chandler sees the mundane life he leads and briefly questions it. The screams of his child that pierce his concentration as he tries to read poetry bring him to a tragic revelation. He knows he is "prisoner" in the house. Little Chandler's fleeting resistance is like a little cloud that passes in the sky. By the end of the story he feels ashamed of his disloyal behavior, completing the circle of emotions, from doubt to assurance to doubt, that he probably will repeat for the rest of his life. The story finishes where it began: with Little Chandler sighing about his unrealized aspirations, but submitting to the melancholy thought that "it was useless to struggle against fortune." Circular routine plagues Chandler as it does for most of the characters in *Dubliners*.

Little Chandler's inability to act on his desires and his dependence on Gallaher to provide experiences he can participate in vicariously make him similar to Lenehan in "Two Gallants." Just as Lenehan stands in Corley's shadow, Little Chandler admires and envies Gallaher. Even when he realizes that Gallaher refuses his invitation to see his home and family out of disinterest, he keeps such sentiments to himself. In Gallaher, an old friend who has done well for himself, Little Chandler sees the hope of escape and success. This friendship sustains Little Chandler's fantasies, allowing him to dream that Gallaher might submit one of his poems to a London paper, and allowing him to feel superior because he has foreign connections. At the same time, as the meeting at the pub progresses, Little Chandler feels cheated by the world since Gallaher can succeed and he cannot, and so once again the friend provides a barometer to measure and judge himself against. Left on his own with his books, Little Chandler must face his own shortcomings.

"COUNTERPARTS"

SUMMARY
In a busy law firm, one of the partners, Mr. Alleyne, angrily orders the secretary to send Farrington to his office. Farrington is a copy clerk in the firm, responsible for making copies of legal documents by hand, and he has failed to produce an important document on time. Mr. Alleyne taunts Farrington and says harshly that if he does not copy the material by closing time his incompetence will be reported to the other partner. This meeting angers Farrington, who mentally makes evening plans to drink with his friends as a respite.

Farrington returns to his desk but is unable to focus on work. He skirts past the chief clerk to sneak out to the local pub where he quickly drinks a beer.

Two clients are speaking with the chief clerk when Farrington returns to the office, making his absence apparent. The clerk asks him to take a file to Mr. Alleyne, who is also with a client. Farrington realizes that the needed file is incomplete because he has failed to copy two letters as requested. Hoping that Mr. Alleyne will not notice, Farrington delivers the incomplete file and returns to his desk to work on his project. Again unable to concentrate, Farrington dreams of hot drinks and crowded pubs, only to realize, with increasing rage, that completing the task is impossible and that he has no hope of getting an advance on his paycheck to fund his thirst. Meanwhile, Mr. Alleyne, having noticed the missing letters, has come to Farrington's desk with his client, the jovial Miss Delacour, and started another abusive critique of Farrington's work. Farrington claims ignorance and wittily insults Mr. Alleyne to the amusement of Miss Delacour and his fellow clerks.

Forced to apologize to Mr. Alleyne, Farrington leaves work without completing his project and dreading the sure backlash at the office. More determined than ever to go to the pub, Farrington pawns his pocket watch for drinking money. At his first stop he meets his friends Nosey Flynn, O'Halloran, and Paddy Leonard, and tells them of his shining moment insulting his boss. Another clerk from the office arrives and joins them, repeating the story. Soon the men leave the pub, and O'Halloran, Leonard, and Farrington move on to another place. There Leonard introduces the men to an acrobat named Weathers, who happily accepts the drinks the other men buy for him. Farrington becomes irritated at the amount of money he spends, but the men keep drinking and move to yet another pub. Weathers meets the men there and Farrington begrudgingly buys him another drink out of courtesy. Farrington's frustrations build as he flirts with an elegant woman sitting nearby who ultimately ignores his advances. Leonard and O'Halloran then convince Farrington to arm wrestle with Weathers, who has been boasting about his strength to the men. After two attempts, Farrington loses.

Filled with rage and humiliation, Farrington travels home to Shelbourne Road, a lower-middle-class area southeast of the city center. Entering his dark house, he calls to his wife Ada but is met by one of his five children, his son Tom. When Tom informs him that Ada is at church, Farrington orders Tom to light up the house and prepare dinner for him. He then realizes that the house fire has been left to burn out, which means his dinner will be long in coming. With his anger at boiling point, Farrington begins to beat Tom, who plaintively promises to say a Hail Mary for Farrington if he stops.

ANALYSIS

While many characters in *Dubliners* desire something, face obstacles that frustrate them, and ultimately forfeit their desires in paralysis, Farrington sees everything in the world as an obstacle to his comfort and never relents in his vitriol. The tedium of work irritates Farrington first, but so does everything he encounters in the story. The root of Farrington's violent and explosive behavior is the circular experience of routine and repetition that defines his life. Farrington's job is based on duplication—he copies documents for a demanding boss. His job, in other words, is to produce replications of other things, and the monotony of this job enrages him. Farrington envisions release from such deadening activity in the warmth and drink of public houses, but his experiences there only beget further routine. He repeats the story of the confrontation with Mr. Alleyne to his friends, who then also repeat it. Following the "round" tradition in which each person in a group takes turns buying drinks for all companions present, he continually spends money and consumes more alcohol. The presence of Weathers, who takes advantage of this system, makes Farrington realize how such tradition and repetition literally rob him. His anger mounts throughout the story.

Farrington hurtles forward in the story without pausing to think about his actions or why he feels such discontent. As a result, his circular activities become more and more brutal. When he loses two arm wrestling matches to Weathers, a "mere boy," he goes home only to beat his own boy. What begins as mundane copying, the story hints, spins out of control into a cycle of brutal abuse. While other characters in the collection acknowledge their routine lives, struggle, then accept their fate passively, Farrington is unaware and unrelenting. The title, "Counterparts," refers to a copy or duplicate of a legal paper, the stuff of Farrington's career, but also to things that are similar or equal to each other. Farrington lives a life of counterparts, to dangerous ends. His pawning of his watch may symbolically release him from the shackles of schedules and time demands, but the frustrations of work only take on new and more extreme forms at the pub and at home. For Farrington, life repeats itself:

work is like the pub is like home. As "Counterparts" illustrates, this bleeding between different areas of life inevitably exists. When maddening routine and repetition form the backbone of experience, passivity may result, but so too might volatile frustration.

The abuse that other stories in *Dubliners* allude to becomes explicit in "Counterparts," and the consistent emotional theme of anger underpins every event in the story. Joyce uses adjectives like *heavy*, *dark*, and *dirty* to describe Farrington—he is quite literally worn out by frustration and anger. Not even the desperate servitude and piety of his son touch him, signaling that spirituality fails to save and protect. Farrington is unable to realize that his own actions are far worse than the mocking cruelty of his boss. Joyce refers to Farrington both by his name and as "the man" throughout the story. In one sentence he is the familiar character of Farrington that the reader follows throughout the story, yet in another he is "the man" on the street, on the train, in an office. Farrington, in a sense, acts as an exchangeable or general type, both a specific man and everyman. Joyce's fluid way of addressing him thus serves to weave Farrington into the Dublin streetscape and suggest that his brutality is nothing unusual.

"CLAY"

SUMMARY

Maria, a maid at a Protestant charity that houses troubled women, proudly reviews her preparation for Halloween festivities at her workplace. Running through the evening's schedule, she also looks forward to her celebrations for later in the night with the family of a friend, Joe Donnelly. Maria nursed Joe and his brother, Alphy, when they were young, and both of them helped Maria get her present job. Though Maria was at first uncomfortable with the Protestant association of the charity, she has grown to accept it and is warmly loved by the staff and residents. The time for festivities arrives, and Maria distributes the seasonal spiced bread, called barmbrack, and tea. One of the women raises a toast to Maria.

Afterwards, Maria prepares for her journey to Joe's home, admiring her appearance in the mirror before leaving her room. On her way to Joe's, Maria does some shopping. Moving through the crowded streets, she visits two shops to buy cakes for the children and a special plum cake for Joe and his wife. She boards a crowded tram and sits next to a "colonel-looking gentleman" who kindly makes room for her. They chat casually during the ride, and at Maria's stop they cordially say goodbye to each other.

At Joe's home, the Donnellys happily greet Maria. She distributes the sweets to the children, but when she goes to present to plum cake to Joe and his wife, she cannot find the package. Maria desperately looks everywhere, with no success. The Donnellys suggest that she probably left it on the tram, which makes Maria think about the man, and she scolds herself for getting distracted by his presence and for ruining her own surprise gift. Joe consoles Maria by telling her stories about his office and offering nuts and wine.

The conversation turns to the past, and Maria tries to say good things about Alphy. The brothers have had a falling out, though Joe has named his eldest son after Alphy. Joe grows defensive, and his wife attempts to divert the matter by starting a round of traditional Halloween games. Two girls from the house next door help the children to arrange a table of saucers filled with different objects and lead a blindfolded Maria over to them. Maria touches the saucer with a mound of wet clay on it, which in games of this sort represents early death. Joe's wife reproves the visiting girls, as though clay should not be an option given its bad omen. Maria reaches again and touches a prayer book, forecasting a pious life in a convent.

The festivities continue happily until Joe asks Maria to sing for the family. With Mrs. Donnelly at the piano, Maria timidly sings "I Dreamt that I Dwelt," a popular opera aria written by an Irish nineteenth-century composer. Maria sings the first stanza twice, but no one points out her mistake. Joe is visibly moved to tears and, to cover up his reaction, asks his wife where the corkscrew is.

SUMMARY & ANALYSIS

ANALYSIS

Unlike the female protagonists in earlier stories, Maria does not confront decisions and situations with large consequences, but rather those whose consequences seem small or even nonexistent. Nothing much seems to happen in this story, and its inaction stands out even more since it follows the violent "Counterparts" in the collection. Maria illustrates the quiet life of a single maid, whose spotless reputation as "a veritable peace-maker" attests to her placid lifestyle. The excitement with which the Donnelly family greets her shows that outside of work she is equally loved. Maria is a small, gentle woman whose continuous laughter brings the tip of her nose to touch her chin—as though she loses herself in her joy. However, the events in "Clay," though quiet, are far from innocuous. Even

Maria, with her serene life, harbors unhappiness and frustration, and instead of being exempt from the tedium of routine, she is in fact entrenched in it.

Maria has such little conflict and so few varied experiences that the smallest details of daily living have become the focus of her energies, and these details deaden her life. For Maria, everything demands organization and precision. She fastidiously supervises the distribution of food portions at the charity, she prides herself on her neat and tidy body, and she repeatedly divides up the minutes she will schedule for traveling and shopping for the evening at Joe's. Maria intends for her attention to minute details to create order and clarity in her life, but such rigidity actually encourages frustration and emotional reactions that are out of proportion to the situation at hand. When she realizes that she has misplaced the plum cake, she is so furious with herself and her carelessness that she almost cries. Unlike Eveline, who feels numb to the loss of her lover and a potential new life, Maria feels acute emotions over events that are far more trivial. "Clay" demonstrates that Maria's responses are just as restraining as Eveline's. Maria most likely focuses intently on life's small details in order to avoid greater pains. Joe exhibits the same behavior: He covers up his mysterious, tearful reaction to Maria's song by asking his wife to show him where an ordinary household item is. Preoccupation with such trivial matters helps to repress the more difficult aspects of life. The reader never knows what moves Joe, nor what Maria might feel on deeper levels.

The title "Clay" draws attention to Maria's fateful selection of clay in the Halloween game and applies that symbolism of early death to the story as a whole. Rather than implying a literal death, the clay casts Maria's uneventful, detail-oriented life as a metaphorical early death. Clay also suggests the state of Maria and her life up to that moment. Like the paralytic Father Flynn from "The Sisters," Maria hovers in a state between living and dying where engagement with her surroundings cannot move beyond a superficial, material level. Like Farrington in "Counterparts," she fails to recognize the tedious routine of her days, as her repetition of the song suggests. Maria does not actively shape her experience in significant ways, but instead she allows it to shape her. The image of her face collapsing into itself in laughter implies that Maria in her blind happiness is moldable and soft, like clay. Maria chooses the prayer book after the clay, which suggests she might find escape in the cloistered life of a convent. Whether Maria escapes or not, some part of her will die.

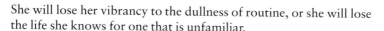

She will lose her vibrancy to the dullness of routine, or she will lose the life she knows for one that is unfamiliar.

"A Painful Case"

> *He looked down the slope and, at the base, in the shadow of the wall of the Park, he saw some human figures lying. Those venal and furtive loves filled him with despair. He gnawed the rectitude of his life; he felt that he had been outcast from life's feast.*
> *(See* Quotations*, p. 67)*

Summary

A predictable, unadventurous bank cashier, Mr. Duffy lives an existence of prudence and organization. He keeps a tidy house, eats at the same restaurants, and makes the same daily commute. Occasionally, Mr. Duffy allows himself an evening out at the opera or a concert, and on one of these evenings he engages in a conversation with another audience member, Mrs. Sinico, a striking woman who sits with her young daughter. Subsequent encounters ensue at other concerts, and on the third occasion Mr. Duffy sets up a time and day to meet purposely with her. Because Mrs. Sinico is married and her husband, a captain of a merchant ship, is constantly away from home, Mr. Duffy feels slightly uncomfortable with the clandestine nature of the relationship. Nevertheless, they continue to meet, always at her home.

Their discussions revolve around their similar intellectual interests, including books, political theories, and music, and with each meeting they draw more closely together. Such sharing gradually softens Mr. Duffy's hard character. However, during one of their meetings, Mrs. Sinico takes Mr. Duffy's hand and places it on her cheek, which deeply bothers Mr. Duffy. He feels Mrs. Sinico has misinterpreted his acts of companionship as sexual advances. In response, he cuts off the relationship, first by stopping his visits and then by arranging a final meeting at a cake shop in Dublin, deliberately not at Mrs. Sinico's home. They agree to end the relationship, but Mrs. Sinico's emotional presence at this meeting suggests she is less willing to say goodbye than is Mr. Duffy.

Four years pass. One evening, during his usual dinner in town, Mr. Duffy reads a newspaper article that surprises him enough to halt his eating and hurry home. There, he reads the article, entitled

"A Painful Case," once more. The article recounts the death of Mrs. Sinico, who was hit by a train at a station in Dublin the previous evening. Witness accounts and the coroner's inquest deem that the death was caused by shock or heart failure, and not injuries from the train itself. The article also explains that Mrs. Sinico was a drinker and had become increasingly detached from her husband over the past two years. The article concludes with the statement that no one is responsible for her death.

The news of Mrs. Sinico's death at first angers but later saddens Mr. Duffy. Perhaps suspecting suicide or weakness in character, he feels disgusted by her death and by his connection to her life. Disturbed, he leaves his home to visit a local pub, where he drinks and remembers his relationship with her. His anger begins to subside, and by the time he leaves to walk home, he feels deep remorse, mainly for ending the relationship and losing the potential for companionship it offered. Upon seeing a pair of lovers in the park by his home, Mr. Duffy realizes that he gave up the only love he'd experienced in life. He feels utterly alone.

ANALYSIS

Because Mr. Duffy cannot tolerate unpredictability, his relationship with Mrs. Sinico is a disruption to his orderly life that he knows he must eliminate, but which he ultimately fails to control. Mrs. Sinico awakens welcome new emotions in Mr. Duffy, but when she makes an intimate gesture he reacts with surprise and rigidity. Though all along he spoke of the impossibility of sharing one's self and the inevitability of loneliness, Mrs. Sinico's gesture suggests that another truth exists, and this truth frightens Mr. Duffy. Accepting Mrs. Sinico's offered truth, which opens the possibility for love and deep feeling, would mean changing his life entirely, which Mr. Duffy cannot do. He resumes his solitary life with some relief. When Mr. Duffy reads of Mrs. Sinico's death four years later, he reacts with shock and disgust, as he did when Mrs. Sinico touched his hand. Mrs. Sinico's dramatic demise points to a depth of feeling she possessed that Mr. Duffy will never understand or share, and it provides Mr. Duffy with an epiphany as he walks home. He realizes that his concern with order and rectitude shut her out of his life, and that this concern excludes him from living fully. Like other characters in *Dubliners* who experience epiphanies, Mr. Duffy is not inspired to begin a new phase in his life, but instead he bitterly accepts his loneliness.

"A Painful Case" concludes where it begins, with Mr. Duffy alone. This narrative circle mimics the many routines that comprise Mr. Duffy's life and deny him true companionship. The story opens with a detailed depiction of Mr. Duffy's unadorned home in a neighborhood he chose for its distance from the hustle and bustle of Dublin. Colors are limited and walls are bare in Mr. Duffy's house, and disorder, spontaneity, and passion are unwelcome. As such, Mr. Duffy's house serves as a microcosm of his soul. His regulatory impulses make each day the same as the next. Such deadening repetitiveness ultimately brings Mr. Duffy death in life: the death of someone who once stirred his longings to be with others. In life, Mrs. Sinico invigorated Mr. Duffy's routine and, through her intimacy, came close to warming his cold heart. Only in death, however, does she succeed in revealing his cycle of solitude to him. The tragedy of this story is threefold. First, Mr. Duffy must face a dramatic death before he can rethink his lifestyle and outlook. Second, acknowledging the problems in his lifestyle makes him realize his culpability: Mrs. Sinico died of a broken heart that he caused. Third, and perhaps most tragic, Mr. Duffy will not change the life he has created for himself. He is paralyzed, despite his revelations and his guilt.

Joyce's choice of symbolic names in "A Painful Case" articulates the story's somber subject of thwarted love and loneliness. Duffy derives from the Irish word for dark, suggesting the grim, solemn mood in which the story unfolds and Mr. Duffy lives. The suburb in which Mr. Duffy resides, Chapelizod, takes its name from the French, Chapel d'Iseult. Iseult is half of the famed set of lovers, Tristan and Iseult, whose doomed affair ranks as one of the most iconic love stories in literature and music. This name's appearance in the story as Mr. Duffy's home neighborhood, which he purposely chose in order to distance himself from Dublin's hustle and bustle and which is the starting point for his daily routine, connects the unrequited love and death of Mrs. Sinico with Mr. Duffy's restrained existence.

"Ivy Day in the Committee Room"

Summary
On Ivy Day, a group of political canvassers working for a mayoral candidate in the city council elections gather in the National Party committee room to warm up from the cold, drink together, talk politics, and await their wage payment. Ivy Day, October 6, commem-

orates the politician Charles Stuart Parnell's death in 1891, and Parnell's presence pervades this story. Mat O'Connor, one of the canvassers, sits and smokes as Old Jack, the porter of the building, tends to a dwindling fire and tells O'Connor about his son. Both men are employed by Richard Tierney, a pub owner who is running for the office of Lord Mayor in the upcoming elections. Another man, Joe Hynes, joins the two men, but he does not work for Tierney. He is deeply critical of the candidate, suspecting him of being sympathetic to the British even though he runs as a Nationalist, the party that supports an independent Ireland. Another canvasser, John Henchy, also joins the group. He coolly acknowledges the presence of Hynes and reviews the day's campaigning efforts with O'Connor before he too launches into a critique of the candidate, though for his tardiness in paying employees like himself rather than the candidate's political leanings.

Hynes leaves, and following his exit Henchy expresses his suspicions that Hynes is an informer for Colgan, the working-class candidate running against Tierney. O'Connor gently deflects the comment, but, encouraged by Old Jack, Henchy continues with his conspiracy theory that such informers probably work for the British. He makes a connection between Hynes and the infamous Henry Charles Sirr, an Irishman who, as an officer in the British Army, helped to suppress Irish uprisings against the British in the late eighteenth and early nineteenth centuries. Another man, Father Keon, soon appears in the doorway looking for someone who is not in the room, and scurries off to Tierney's pub to find the man. Henchy and O'Connor chat about the priest, who has a reputation for being a "black sheep," unattached to any church or institution.

The men then turn the talk to drink, and Henchy complains that Tierney had promised to send some stout to the room that has yet to arrive. Soon thereafter, though, a boy appears bearing bottles from the pub, and Henchy exclaims that Tierney keeps to his word. Two more canvassers named Crofton and Lyons arrive. Henchy turns the discussion back to politics, making clear his support of Tierney's catch-all approach of supporting "whatever will benefit his country," even the welcome of the English king, which, he argues, would boost the local economy. O'Connor counterargues, noting that the National Party under Parnell would never place capital over political theory, a point that Henchy meets with a simple "Parnell is dead." Lyons backs O'Connor, as does Crofton, spurring Henchy to laud Parnell as well. At this moment, Hynes returns, and O'Connor

asks him to read a poem he wrote, entitled "The Death of Parnell." The poem celebrates Parnell and paints him as a man betrayed by treachery. All of the men applaud the recitation.

ANALYSIS

"Ivy Day in the Committee Room" mourns the state of Irish politics and people's inability to maintain consistent beliefs. The group of men gathering in the once-active and promising room of the National Party, which used to be Parnell's headquarters, show little enthusiasm for the candidate they apparently support, but instead bicker about trivial things. The "Committee Room" in the title connects this scene of atrophy to the betrayal of Parnell. The Committee Room in London was where Irish politicians chose not to support Parnell as a leader in December 1890. This event destroyed Parnell's career, and, this story suggests, the morale and hopes of the next generation as well. Yet these men, particularly Henchy, demonstrate wavering beliefs that show they too are guilty of betrayal. "Ivy Day in the Committee Room" reveals how the past shapes the present, but also how those living in the present fail to correct or atone for past wrongs.

The men in the story dwell on the past so much that almost no constructive action takes place. The story opens with Old Jack telling O'Connor about his drunken, disloyal son, which from a broader perspective suggests that the political successors to Parnell do just that to their political "father": complicate and disregard rather than support. The commemorative title of the story highlights that on this special day, these men remain inactive. Ivy Day honors Parnell's death and takes its name from the loyal Dubliners who, at Parnell's funeral, wore the ivy growing by his grave in their lapels. In the story, both O'Connor and Hynes wear ivy in memory of Parnell, but they involve themselves only in petty politics, if they involve themselves at all. Hynes turns up in the room to critique Tierney and plant seeds of dissent, and O'Connor shrugs off his job. He canvasses—or, rather, fails to canvass—for a candidate he seems to care little about, since he sits inside to avoid promoting in the inclement weather. O'Connor also lights his cigarettes by burning the information cards he is meant to hand out, even when offered a match. His dedication to supporting Tierney, the new Nationalist candidate, could not be any weaker.

The men in the committee room, the story suggests, are paralyzed in a cycle of inactivity and equivocation. Henchy, by far the worst offender, harshly criticizes Tierney, whom he calls "Tricky Dicky," and also supports him energetically. Henchy continually switches his allegiance. At one moment he bemoans Tierney's empty promise to send beer, while in the next moment he defends Tierney's sense of honor and recites his promotional speech, in which he lauds Tierney for being attached to no political party. The appearance of Father Keon indicates that this inability to devote oneself to a cause also applies to religion. Looking like "a poor clergyman or a poor actor," this ambivalent, ambiguous figure hovers on the threshold of the door, neither committing himself to the room nor removing himself from it. The priest, unattached to any church and uncertain of where he stands, suggests the distrust that exists in any belief system, whether spiritual or political. The story, set in the wake of Irish political collapse, hints that uncertainty defines the times.

Hynes's poetic recitation is the one moment of tribute in the story, and it stirs the men into quiet reflection on their unremarkable contribution to politics. After they applaud Hynes, the men sit in silence, respect, and, perhaps, guilt. Hynes's words, however grandiose, call for Parnell's spirit to rise again in Ireland, but the men of "Ivy Day in the Committee Room" realize at this moment that they are not the ones to lead the charge. Instead, they will sit year after year, impotently wearing their ivy. The story mourns the death of Parnell, but it also mourns the death of firm political opinion in general.

"A MOTHER"

They thought they had only a girl to deal with and that, therefore, they could ride roughshod over her. But she would show them their mistake. They wouldn't have dared to have treated her like that if she had been a man. But she would see that her daughter got her rights: she wouldn't be fooled.

(See QUOTATIONS, p. 70)

SUMMARY

As the assistant secretary to the *Eire Abu*, or "Ireland to Victory," Society, Mr. Holohan tries to organize a series of concerts showcasing local musicians. He finally visits Mrs. Kearney, whose eldest daughter Kathleen has a reputation in Dublin as a talented pianist and exemplary speaker of Irish. Kathleen studies the piano and French in a convent school like Mrs. Kearney did, and she receives tutoring in Irish at the insistence of her mother as well. Mrs. Kearney is not surprised when Mr. Holohan proposes that Kathleen perform as an accompanist in the series, and she advises Mr. Holohan in drawing up a contract to secure a payment of eight guineas for Kathleen's performance in the four concerts. Given Mr. Holohan's inexperience in organizing such an event, she also helps him to lay out the program and complete other duties.

After her efforts, Mrs. Kearney is disturbed when the concerts turn out to be sub-par for her high standards. The first two concerts are poorly attended, the audience members behave "indecorously," and many of the artists are mediocre. Mrs. Kearney complains to Mr. Holohan, but neither he nor the head secretary, Mr. Fitzpatrick, appear bothered by the turnout. Nevertheless, the Society's committee cancels the third concert in hopes that doing so will boost attendance for the final one. This change in plans infuriates Mrs. Kearney, who already has become aggravated by the men's lax attitudes and what she sees as loose manners. She approaches Mr. Holohan and insists that such a change should not alter the contracted payment, but Mr. Holohan only refers her to Mr. Fitzpatrick, who also dodges her inquiries.

On the night of the final concert, Mrs. Kearney, accompanied by her husband and Kathleen, arrives early at the performance hall to meet the men, but neither Mr. Holohan nor Mr. Fitzpatrick has arrived. As the musicians gather and await curtain call, Mrs. Kearney paces in the dressing room until finally she finds Mr. Holohan and, following him to a quiet hallway, pursues the issue of the contract. Again he insists that such matters are not his "business" and that she must consult Mr. Fitzpatrick. Enraged, she returns to the dressing room, where the musicians wait for Kathleen to join them so they can start the performance, for which the audience loudly clamors. Mrs. Kearney detains her daughter, and when Mr. Holohan arrives to query the delay in performance, she announces that Kathleen will not perform unless paid in full. Mr. Holohan departs in haste and returns with Mr. Fitzpatrick, who gives Mrs. Kearney half of the amount, explaining that the remainder will come at the intermission, after Kathleen's performance. Kathleen plays, during which time the artists and committee members criticize Mrs. Kearney's aggressive conduct. At the intermission, Mr. Fitzpatrick and Mr. Holohan inform Mrs. Kearney that they will pay her daughter the balance after the committee meeting next week. But Mrs. Kearney angrily bickers with Mr. Holohan and finally whisks away her daughter, leaving the concert hall.

ANALYSIS

In "A Mother," Mrs. Kearney's practical but inflexible approach to life, while it gets her what she wants most of the time, ultimately does nothing but increase her own anger. Mrs. Kearney drives herself to accomplish whatever task, challenge, or need is at hand, often without much show of emotion. She marries her husband just to be married, not because of love. In her unyielding insistence that her daughter, Kathleen, receive full payment for her performance, Mrs. Kearney pursues her interests to such a degree that she undoes her own efforts to perfect the concert, and herself. When the organizers provide only half of the fee, Mrs. Kearney embarrasses her daughter and ruins her career by sweeping her out of the concert hall and irritating everyone. Mrs. Kearney is not concerned with a trifling amount of money, she insists, but her rights and her respect. The story leaves the reader guessing why Mrs. Kearney abandons her cause and leaves the concert hall. Is she humiliated? Does she realize that no one shares or sympathizes with her frustrations? Like "an angry stone," Mrs. Kearney will not soften to the circumstances and reconsider. Like other characters in *Dubliners*, she will continue to live according to her own routine.

Through the fastidious character of Mrs. Kearney, "A Mother" subtly critiques shallow concerns about social profile. Mrs. Kearney's immense efforts to organize and perfect are not motivated by an ambition to succeed, the story suggests, but by a concern with status and appearance. She crafts an education for Kathleen of piano, French, and Irish, which makes obvious the family's interest in culture and nationalist efforts. The concert provides Mrs. Kearney with an ideal opportunity to let Kathleen shine as a darling of Irish culture, but her frustrations with the lax society members and her complaints about the venue and selection of artists indicate that Mrs. Kearney obsesses over details to ensure neither Kathleen's happy career nor a successful concert, but her own respected appearance. As more things sully her ideal vision, Mrs. Kearney makes snide observations to herself and struggles to maintain her composure. When she approaches Mr. Fitzpatrick about the contract, she inwardly ridicules his accent, which she perceives to be lower class, but she resists making nasty comments about it, which would "not be ladylike." In the end, Mrs. Kearney's attempt to boost her social appearance results only in her tarnishing it dramatically.

Mrs. Kearney perceives herself as part of a struggle between men and women, noting to herself when she begins to face difficulty with the contract that she would be treated differently if she were a man. This concern briefly places Mrs. Kearney in a sympathetic light and leads the reader to question Mrs. Kearney's circumstances. Yet while Mr. Fitzpatrick and Mr. Holohan appear lazy and uninterested in the concert proceedings, nothing in their actions suggests that they take advantage of Mrs. Kearney. In fact, they struggle to provide the demanded payment for Kathleen. Like Mrs. Mooney in "The Boarding House," a female protagonist challenges the reader to consider her plight in a larger social context. Mrs. Kearney wants to ensure her adequate rights, but she also must appear ladylike— for her, the combination is incompatible.

"GRACE"

SUMMARY

A man has fallen down a flight a stairs in a central Dublin pub and is briefly unconscious. Two men and a pub employee carry the man upstairs, and they, along with the manager and the crowd already assembled in the bar, try to figure out what happened. The manager calls a policeman to the scene, but when the officer arrives he offers little help. A bystander succeeds in resuscitating the injured man, who says his name is Tom Kernan. Barely able to answer any questions, Mr. Kernan prepares to leave when a friend of his, Jack Power, emerges from the crowd and escorts him to a carriage. During the ride home, Mr. Kernan shows Mr. Power that he injured his tongue in the fall, and as such is unable to speak and explain the accident. This event reflects Mr. Kernan's recent fortunes: he used to be an esteemed businessman but has recently hit a rough patch. After the carriage arrives at the house and Mr. Kernan goes to bed, Mr. Power chats with the children and Mrs. Kernan. He mentally notes to himself the lower-class accents of the children, just as Mrs. Kernan begins to lament her husband's neglectful behavior. Mr. Power assures her that he will help Mr. Kernan to reform.

The final and third section of "Grace" occurs at the Jesuit Church service and focuses on the words of the officiating priest, Father Purdon. Mr. Cunningham, Mr. Kernan, Mr. M'Coy, Mr. Power, and Mr. Fogarty sit near each other in the pews, which are filled with men from all walks of Dublin life, including pawnbrokers and newspaper report-ers. From the red-lit pulpit, Father Purdon preaches to them, he claims, as businessman to businessman, as the "spiritual accountant" to the congregation before him. The service, in turn, is a chance for reckon-ing, and he asks the men to tally up their sins and compare them to their clean or guilty consciences. Both those whose accounts balance and those whose show discrepancies will be saved by God's grace, as long as they strive to rectify their faults.After two nights, a group of Mr. Ker-nan's friends visit the house in order to convince Mr. Kernan to join them in a Catholic retreat, or cleansing service. The challenge lies in the fact that Mr. Kernan is a former Protestant who converted to Catholi-cism for his wife and has never warmly accepted his new church. Mr. Power, Mr. Cunningham, and Mr. M'Coy spend their visit at first talk-ing about Mr. Kernan's accident and his health, taking time to com-plain about the ineffective policeman at the bar. Then they gradually reveal their plans for the retreat and turn the discussion to religion. Mr. Fogarty, who runs a neighboring grocery, joins the group, and they all praise the Irish priesthood and nineteenth-century popes. Mr. Kernan follows along, contributes, and eventually agrees to join the retreat, with one exception: he refuses to light any candles as part of the service, explaining that he does not believe in magic.

ANALYSIS

In "Grace," a framework of fall, conversion, and redemption reveals the complicated role of religion in Dubliners' lives. The three separate sections of the narrative serve to undermine the process of redemption. In the first section, Mr. Kernan serves, quite literally, as the "fallen man." His disastrous accident at the pub apparently is part of a downward spiral he has been experiencing and remains a mystery in the story. Mr. Kernan can remember only that he was with two men in the bar, but claims no other recollection of the event. Mr. Kernan probably hides the truth out of embarrassment, forcing the reader to pull together the hints that suggest he was drunk and abandoned by his companions. This puzzling start to the story makes the steadfast efforts of Mr. Kernan's friends to help him all the more strange. We don't know what's wrong with Mr. Kernan or why he needs help. The story complicates this seeming goodwill by revealing the unsupportive tendencies of friends like Mr. Power, who inwardly grimaces about the lower-class upbringing of the Kernan chil-dren. That Mr. Power recoils from certain status signs suggests that his concern for others stems from his concern for his own reputation.

The second section of the narrative treats Mr. Kernan's conversion, and Joyce undermines this process by showing the men attempting to convince Mr. Kernan to join the retreat with inaccurate details about Catholic church history. The men discuss the supposedly unspotted history of the Jesuits, trying to boost Mr. Kernan's view of the church, and deflect Mr. Kernan's complaint about provincial priests by claiming that "[t]he Irish priesthood is honoured all the world over." When Mr. Fogarty arrives, the men begin to discuss the illuminated career of the nineteenth-century Pope Leo XIII, but they do so by misusing a variety of Latin terms. Mr. Cunningham, by far the most verbose of the group, attempts to recount the Church debate over papal infallibility, but he makes mistakes as well. The point of the scene is not the specific errors, but the men's reliance on big terms and names to make themselves appear serious and pious. As such, Mr. Kernan's conversion is something of a sham.

Mr. Kernan's "cleansing" in the final section of the narrative never really occurs. He arrives at the church and listens to the priest, but the story does not follow his rise from the fall. Instead, the many contradictions in the service are highlighted, which serves to critique the church as a place of healing. Father Purdon shares his name with the name of the street that is home to the red-light district, or prostitution area, of Dublin, and his pulpit shines with a red light as though he is a beacon of sin, not redemption. The progression in the story from fall to redemption, then, stalls and halts. "Grace" seems to ask how far indeed is the distance between the bottom of the stairs in the pub and the pews in the church.

The conclusion of the story assures the men that grace can save them from sin, but the word *grace* has multiple meanings. It can refer to the quality of poise or politeness. It can also refer to a granted delay or postponement, such as a grace period given to a debtor who owes money. It might sometimes refer to the unconditional favor of God granted to humans that enables them to be saved. All of these meanings surface to some extent in this story and serve to point out how simple events become infused with spiritual significance, and not always to useful ends. Mr. Kernan himself embodies the word *grace* ironically, as he is literally a man who has no poise. His friends, however, interpret this fall as indicating a lack of God's grace. The story concludes with Father Purdon's assurance that even the fallen man can be saved with the help of God's grace, but the priest uses the economic language of accounting to communicate his thoughts to the congregation of businessmen. Reckoning with oneself, then, acts as a period of grace, yet none of the men in the story come to terms with themselves. Searching for grace becomes yet another repetitive cycle for these Dubliners.

"THE DEAD"

Yes, the newspapers were right: snow was general all over Ireland. It was falling on every part of the dark central plain, on the treeless hills, falling softly upon the Bog of Allen and, farther westward, softly falling into the dark mutinous Shannon waves. It was falling, too, upon every part of the lonely churchyard on the hill where Michael Furey lay buried.

(See QUOTATIONS, p. 66)

SUMMARY

At the annual dance and dinner party held by Kate and Julia Morkan and their young niece, Mary Jane Morkan, the housemaid Lily frantically greets guests. Set at or just before the feast of the Epiphany on January 6, which celebrates the manifestation of Christ's divinity to the Magi, the party draws together a variety of relatives and friends. Kate and Julia particularly await the arrival of their favorite nephew, Gabriel Conroy, and his wife, Gretta. When they arrive, Gabriel attempts to chat with Lily as she takes his coat, but she snaps in reply to his question about her love life. Gabriel ends the uncomfortable exchange by giving Lily a generous tip, but the experience makes him anxious. He relaxes when he joins his aunts and Gretta, though Gretta's good-natured teasing about his dedication to galoshes irritates him. They discuss their decision to stay at a hotel that evening rather than make the long trip home. The arrival of another guest, the always-drunk Freddy Malins, disrupts the conversation. Gabriel makes sure that Freddy is fit to join the party while the guests chat over drinks in between taking breaks from the dancing. An older gentleman, Mr. Browne, flirts with some young girls, who dodge his advances. Gabriel steers a drunken Freddy toward the drawing room to get help from Mr. Browne, who attempts to sober Freddy up.

The party continues with a piano performance by Mary Jane. More dancing follows, which finds Gabriel paired up with Miss Ivors, a fellow university instructor. A fervent supporter of Irish culture, Miss Ivors embarrasses Gabriel by labeling him a "West Briton" for writing literary reviews for a conservative newspaper.

Gabriel dismisses the accusation, but Miss Ivors pushes the point by inviting Gabriel to visit the Aran Isles, where Irish is spoken, during the summer. When Gabriel declines, explaining that he has arranged a cycling trip on the continent, Miss Ivors corners him about his lack of interest in his own country. Gabriel exclaims that he is sick of Ireland. After the dance, he flees to a corner and engages in a few more conversations, but he cannot forget the interlude with Miss Ivors.

Just before dinner, Julia sings a song for the guests. Miss Ivors makes her exit to the surprise of Mary Jane and Gretta, and to the relief of Gabriel. Finally, dinner is ready, and Gabriel assumes his place at the head of the table to carve the goose. After much fussing, everyone eats, and finally Gabriel delivers his speech, in which he praises Kate, Julia, and Mary Jane for their hospitality. Framing this quality as an Irish strength, Gabriel laments the present age in which such hospitality is undervalued. Nevertheless, he insists, people must not linger on the past and the dead, but live and rejoice in the present with the living. The table breaks into a loud applause for Gabriel's speech, and the entire party toasts their three hostesses.

Later, guests begin to leave, and Gabriel recounts a story about his grandfather and his horse, which forever walked in circles even when taken out of the mill where it worked. After finishing the anecdote, Gabriel realizes that Gretta stands transfixed by the song that Mr. Bartell D'Arcy sings in the drawing room. When the music stops and the rest of the party guests assemble before the door to leave, Gretta remains detached and thoughtful. Gabriel is enamored with and preoccupied by his wife's mysterious mood and recalls their courtship as they walk from the house and catch a cab into Dublin.

At the hotel, Gabriel grows irritated by Gretta's behavior. She does not seem to share his romantic inclinations, and in fact bursts into tears. Gretta confesses that she has been thinking of the song from the party because a former lover had sung it to her in her youth in Galway. Gretta recounts the sad story of this boy, Michael Furey, who died after waiting outside of her window in the cold. Gretta later falls asleep, but Gabriel remains awake, disturbed by Gretta's new information. He curls up on the bed, contemplating his own mortality. Seeing the snow at the window, he envisions it blanketing the graveyard where Michael Furey rests, as well as all of Ireland.

Analysis

In "The Dead," Gabriel Conroy's restrained behavior and his reputation with his aunts as the nephew who takes care of everything mark him as a man of authority and caution, but two encounters with women at the party challenge his confidence. First, Gabriel clumsily provokes a defensive statement from the overworked Lily when he asks her about her love life. Instead of apologizing or explaining what he meant, Gabriel quickly ends the conversation by giving Lily a holiday tip. He blames his prestigious education for his inability to relate to servants like Lily, but his willingness to let money speak for him suggests that he relies on the comforts of his class to maintain distance. The encounter with Lily shows that Gabriel, like his aunts, cannot tolerate a "back answer," but he is unable to avoid such challenges as the party continues. During his dance with Miss Ivors, he faces a barrage of questions about his nonexistent nationalist sympathies, which he doesn't know how to answer appropriately. Unable to compose a full response, Gabriel blurts out that he is sick of his own country, surprising Miss Ivors and himself with his unmeasured response and his loss of control.

Gabriel's unease culminates in his tense night with Gretta, and his final encounter with her ultimately forces him to confront his stony view of the world. When he sees Gretta transfixed by the music at the end of the party, Gabriel yearns intensely to have control of her strange feelings. Though Gabriel remembers their romantic courtship and is overcome with attraction for Gretta, this attraction is rooted not in love but in his desire to control her. At the hotel, when Gretta confesses to Gabriel that she was thinking of her first love, he becomes furious at her and himself, realizing that he has no claim on her and will never be "master." After Gretta falls asleep, Gabriel softens. Now that he knows that another man preceded him in Gretta's life, he feels not jealousy, but sadness that Michael Furey once felt an aching love that he himself has never known. Reflecting on his own controlled, passionless life, he realizes that life is short, and those who leave the world like Michael Furey, with great passion, in fact live more fully than people like himself.

The holiday setting of Epiphany emphasizes the profoundness of Gabriel's difficult awakening that concludes the story and the collection. Gabriel experiences an inward change that makes him examine his own life and human life in general. While many characters in *Dubliners* suddenly stop pursuing what they desire without explanation, this story offers more specific articulation for Gabriel's actions. Gabriel sees himself as a shadow of a person, flickering in a world in which the living and the dead meet. Though in his speech at the dinner he insisted on the division between the past of the dead and the present of the living, Gabriel now recognizes, after hearing that Michael Furey's memory lives on, that such division is false. As he looks out of his hotel window, he sees the falling snow, and he imagines it covering Michael Furey's grave just as it covers those people still living, as well as the entire country of Ireland. The story leaves open the possibility that Gabriel might change his attitude and embrace life, even though his somber dwelling on the darkness of Ireland closes *Dubliners* with morose acceptance. He will eventually join the dead and will not be remembered.

The Morkans' party consists of the kind of deadening routines that make existence so lifeless in *Dubliners*. The events of the party repeat each year: Gabriel gives a speech, Freddy Malins arrives drunk, everyone dances the same memorized steps, everyone eats. Like the horse that circles around and around the mill in Gabriel's anecdote, these Dubliners settle into an expected routine at this party. Such tedium fixes the characters in a state of paralysis. They are unable to break from the activities that they know, so they live life without new experiences, numb to the world. Even the food on the table evokes death. The life-giving substance appears at "rival ends" of the table that is lined with parallel rows of various dishes, divided in the middle by "sentries" of fruit and watched from afar by "three squads of bottles." The military language transforms a table set for a communal feast into a battlefield, reeking with danger and death.

"The Dead" encapsulates the themes developed in the entire collection and serves as a balance to the first story, "The Sisters." Both stories piercingly explore the intersection of life and death and cast a shadow over the other stories. More than any other story, however, "The Dead" squarely addresses the state of Ireland in this respect. In his speech, Gabriel claims to lament the present age in which hospitality like that of the Morkan family is undervalued, but at the same time he insists that people must not linger on the past, but embrace the present. Gabriel's words betray him, and he ultimately encourages a tribute to the past, the past of hospitality, that lives on in the present party. His later thoughts reveal this attachment to the past when he envisions snow as "general all over Ireland." In every corner of the country, snow touches both the dead and the living, uniting them in frozen paralysis. However, Gabriel's thoughts in the final lines of *Dubliners* suggest that the living might in fact be able to free themselves and live unfettered by deadening routines and the past. Even in January, snow is unusual in Ireland and cannot last forever.

Important Quotations Explained

1. Yes, the newspapers were right: snow was general all over Ireland. It was falling on every part of the dark central plain, on the treeless hills, falling softly upon the Bog of Allen and, farther westward, softly falling into the dark mutinous Shannon waves. It was falling, too, upon every part of the lonely churchyard on the hill where Michael Furey lay buried.
   —"The Dead"

In the very last paragraph of "The Dead," and hence the last paragraph of *Dubliners*, Gabriel gazes out of his hotel window, watching the falling snow and reflecting on his wife Gretta's recent confession about her childhood love, Michael Furey. Previously in the story, Gabriel had been intoxicated and energized by Gretta's preoccupied mood, which reminded him of their courtship, but her outburst of sobbing undermines his self-assurance. This quiet moment of contemplation portrays Gabriel's muted, hushed acceptance that he was not Gretta's first love, and that in fact he has never felt love at all. The blanket of snow suggests this sense of numbness in Gabriel's character—he is literally frigid to emotion—but also the commonality of this trait. The snow does not fall only outside of Gabriel's window, but, as he envisions it, across the country, from the Harbor of Dublin in the east, to the south in Shannon, and to the west. In other words, everyone, everywhere, is as numb as he is.

In this image, Gabriel also contemplates his mortality, and how his living experience intersects with death and the dead. Snow falls everywhere in Ireland, including on the grave of Michael Furey, who has so recently entered his life. In his speech at his aunts' party, Gabriel had called for the need to live one's life without brooding over the memories of the dead, but here he realizes the futility of such divisions and the lack of feeling they expose in his character. Gretta cannot forget the pain of the dead in her life, and her acute suffering illustrates for Gabriel that the dead are very much a part of the lives around him, including his own. That Gabriel's reflections occur in the nighttime adds to the significance of this quote. As he now broods over the dead, he hovers in that flickering state that separates the vibrancy of one daytime from the next. The darkness above the ground mirrors the darkness beneath the ground, where coffins of the dead rest.

2.   He looked down the slope and, at the base, in the shadow of the wall of the Park, he saw some human figures lying. Those venal and furtive loves filled him with despair. He gnawed the rectitude of his life; he felt that he had been outcast from life's feast.
      —"A Painful Case"

This quote from "A Painful Case" shows Mr. Duffy walking past the park near his home after he has learned of Mrs. Sinico's death. He sees two lovers in the park. They are not specific people, but rather human figures that render the scene universal, and the sight reminds Mr. Duffy of his self-imposed exclusion from companionship. In the story, Mr. Duffy rebukes the intimate gestures of Mrs. Sinico, only to realize here, after her death, how potentially life-changing they could have been. At the same time, the language of this quote articulates Mr. Duffy's relentless spite for such physical expression—it is fleshly and secretive, something that happens in the shadows. This moment enacts a cycle of life and death that echoes throughout *Dubliners*: seeing the living, physical evidence of love in two people leads Mr. Duffy to think of the dead, of Mrs. Sinico, and then to reflect on his own existence. Mr. Duffy's circular thoughts recall the obsessive routines and daily procedures that comprise his life and that make no space for the intimate sharing of love.

The imagery of eating in this quote suggests the importance of reciprocity and union that is so absent in this story. The physical act of eating is an activity that Mr. Duffy attempts to externalize and control. Yet Mr. Duffy must gnaw on his rectitude because he has nothing else and because his rectitude is the root of his exclusion. In living in such a restrained way, including his clockwork, solitary meals at the same establishments, he cannot tolerate the change that love harbors or the emotional output, often so uncontrollable, that it demands. As a result, Mr. Duffy must watch others feast and share in the consumption of the many things the world has to offer, while he remains alone.

QUOTATIONS

3. I watched my master's face pass from amiability to sternness; he hoped I was not beginning to idle. I could not call my wandering thoughts together. I had hardly any patience with the serious work of life which, now that it stood between me and my desire, seemed to me child's play, ugly monotonous child's play.
—"Araby"

In this quote, the young boy of "Araby" has just spoken with Mangan's sister, and now finds himself entirely uninterested and bored by the demands of the classroom. Instead, he thinks of Mangan's sister, of the upcoming bazaar, and of anything but what rests before him. This scene forecasts the boy's future frustration with the tedious details that foil his desires, and it also illustrates the boy's struggle to define himself as an adult, even in the space of the classroom structured as a hierarchy between master and student. Just as mundane lessons obstruct the boy's thoughts, by the end of the story everyday delays undermine his hopes to purchase something for Mangan's sister at the bazaar. In both cases, monotony prevents the boy from fulfilling his desires.

This scene articulates the boy's navigation between childhood and adulthood. He sees the routine boredom of school as child's play—it is easy, unengaging, and repetitive. Desire, on the other hand, is inspirational and liberating. His thoughts, after all, wander everywhere, rather than remain fixed to the place they should be. Yearning for the freedom of adulthood, the boy remains chained to the predictability of childhood. The irony underpinning the word *idle* reflects the hypocrisy of this situation, and as such forms one of the moments in the narrative when the subject's voice speaks through the detached third person. What exactly, the passage asks, is idle about excited desire? Idle activity, rather, defines the activity in school, and thus childhood.

4. He remembered the books of poetry upon his shelves at home. He had bought them in his bachelor days and many an evening, as he sat in the little room of the hall, he had been tempted to take one down from the bookshelf and read out something to his wife. But shyness always held him back; and so the books had remained on their shelves.
—"A Little Cloud"

In this quote from the beginning of "A Little Cloud," Little Chandler sits in his office, waiting for the workday to conclude so he can meet with Gallaher, his old friend. As he thinks about Gallaher's successes as a London newspaper writer, Little Chandler begins to reflect on his own career as a writer. Though he works as a clerk, a job in which writing plays a large part, Little Chandler aspires to be a poet—a writer whose material is human emotion, not drudgery. In this passage, however, Little Chandler dejectedly accepts that such aspirations will never materialize. He has the books, but none of the passionate drive to produce one of his own. The books in the quote, in turn, serve as emblems of Little Chandler's poetic desires. They are present and within reach, but his temerity and hesitation prevent him from pulling them from the shelf. His inability to read to his wife also hints at the contradictory role of marriage in his life: it acts as an inhibitor rather than an encouragement to fulfilling his desires. The final moments of the story confirm this antagonism. Little Chandler musters the courage to read some poetry to himself, but his wife's entry crushes his reverie and makes him feel remorseful for his actions.

The symbolic setting of this passage underscores the competing forces in Little Chandler's life. He wishes to live and write poetically, but does so in the confines of an office space. The imagined presence of the books, juxtaposed with Little Chandler's surroundings, highlights the contrast between his grandiose dreams and the mundane reality that envelops him. Little Chandler's wandering mind evokes the escapist leanings of so many of the characters in *Dubliners*, though his reality at least mimics his dreams. That is, Little Chandler earns his living in a pallid version of the same career about which he fantasizes.

QUOTATIONS

5. They thought they had only a girl to deal with and that, therefore, they could ride roughshod over her. But she would show them their mistake. They wouldn't have dared to have treated her like that if she had been a man. But she would see that her daughter got her rights: she wouldn't be fooled.

—"A Mother"

From "A Mother," this quote reveals the thoughts of Mrs. Kearney toward the end of the final concert in which her daughter, Kathleen, is scheduled to perform. When she agreed to let her daughter participate, Mrs. Kearney arranged a contract in which the organizers agreed to pay Kathleen for three performances. With the second performance cancelled and the third nearly finished, Mrs. Kearney, in the passages before this one, has pursued the organizers of the concert, reminding them that Kathleen must be paid in full despite the changes. Here she expresses her determination in seeing the contract fulfilled—a determination that fixates on the gendered context of the situation. All of the organizers, who have been dodging Mrs. Kearney's inquires, are men. As such, Mrs. Kearney sees her treatment as biased and manipulative. That Mrs. Kearney wants to "show" the men their erred judgment of her fits with Mrs. Kearney's concerns with appearance and performance in the story. Following up with the agreement of the contract isn't enough—she must publicly point out their mistake.

The parallel construction of this quote illustrates on a formal level a confrontational, competitive approach that both bolsters and weakens Mrs. Kearney's quest. The first sentence begins with "they," followed by a sentence that begins with "but she." This move from the critiqued party of men to Mrs. Kearney, a move repeated in the third and fourth sentences, evokes Mrs. Kearney's defensive mindset. "They" may do this, "but *she*" will counter. Such antagonism acts as a rallying cry for Mrs. Kearney, yet it also serves to undercut sympathy for her character. The repeated call for revenge highlights Mrs. Kearney's self-concern that overrides concern for Kathleen. As the progression of the quote indicates, first Mrs. Kearney will valorize herself, and then she will be sure that Kathleen gets paid. Nowhere, however, does the reader hear Kathleen's voice.

KEY FACTS

FULL TITLE
Dubliners

AUTHOR
James Joyce

TYPE OF WORK
Collection of short stories

GENRE
Realist fiction; urban literature

LANGUAGE
English (with some Irish and Hiberno-English sayings)

TIME AND PLACE WRITTEN
Early 1900s, Ireland and Italy

DATE OF FIRST PUBLICATION
1914

PUBLISHER
Grant Richards

NARRATOR
The first three stories are narrated by the main character of each story, which in all three cases is a young, unnamed boy. The rest of the stories are narrated by an anonymous third person who pays close attention to circumstantial detail though in a detached manner.

POINT OF VIEW
The first three stories, told from the first person, focus on the thoughts and observations of the narrators. In the stories told from the third person, the narrators detail objective information and present characters as they would appear to an outsider, but also present thoughts and actions from the protagonists' points of view, giving the reader a sense of what the characters are feeling.

TONE

Though told mainly by an anonymous narrator, the stories of *Dubliners* form a self-conscious examination of Joyce's native city in Ireland. Because the narrator maintains a neutral and distant presence, detecting Joyce's attitude toward his characters is not always easy. The abundance of details about the grim realities of the city and the focus on hardships, however, create a tragic tone and offer a subtle critique.

TENSE

Past tense

SETTING (TIME)

Early 1900s

SETTING (PLACE)

Dublin

MAJOR CONFLICT

Various figures struggle with the challenges of complicated relationships and life in Dublin.

THEMES

The prison of routine; the desire for escape; the intersection of life and death

MOTIFS

Paralysis; epiphany; betrayal; religion

SYMBOLS

Windows; dusk and nighttime; food

FORESHADOWING

The death of Father Flynn in "The Sisters" announces the focus on death in later stories like "The Dead"; story titles hint at events in the stories

KEY FACTS

STUDY QUESTIONS & ESSAY TOPICS

STUDY QUESTIONS

1. *Joyce brings the reader's attention to everyday objects throughout his stories. Discuss some examples and explain the significance of Joyce's use of them in the collection.*

In *Dubliners* Joyce focuses on the restraints that everyday realities impose on important aspects of life, such as relationships. Unremarkable objects thus gain remarkable importance in the characters' lives as symbols of such imposition, and in doing so they illustrate the detrimental impact of the mundane and the routine. In "A Painful Case," for example, Joyce walks the reader through Mr. Duffy's sparsely decorated home. Everyday objects are crucial here because so few of them are present, and the ones that Joyce notes reflect Mr. Duffy's values. Almost everything, such as his furniture and his linens, is black or white, and extremely organized. Mr. Duffy's relationships share similar qualities. He cannot endure the grey, in-between state of his interactions with Mrs. Sinico, nor can he tolerate the messiness of intimacy. In Mr. Duffy's case, objects serve as a microcosm of his person and as a commentary on the loneliness that a preoccupation with detail can harbor. His concern with rectitude may ensure the straightened appearance of his home, but it undermines the possibility of love.

Typical objects also bolster the palpable realism of the stories in the collection. When Joyce describes a character sipping a drink or munching on food, as he does with Lenehan in "Two Gallants," the character becomes real and accessible because of the specific meal he eats and is no longer a distant, abstract figure on the page. Lenehan eats not just dinner, but a dinner of peas and ginger beer. While many of the objects might be unfamiliar to modern or non-Irish readers, they nevertheless create an authenticity that encourages the reader to observe characters closely. Joyce makes the reader privy to all aspects of his characters' lives: both the uneventful necessities and the lofty thoughts, and the connection between the two.

2. *In the first three stories of* DUBLINERS, *Joyce uses first-person narration, though for the rest of the collection he uses third-person. What purpose do the two narrative approaches serve?*

With the first-person narration of "The Sisters," Joyce immediately pulls the reader into the collection. The intimate storytelling of this and the following two stories creates a sense of shared experience: the narrator speaks to the reader as a fellow Dubliner. The transition to the third person in "Eveline" does not necessarily create a detached feeling, but with the rest of the collection the reader becomes a voyeur, watching the ebb and flow of Dublin life as Joyce does. At the same time, Joyce manages to include the same sort of intimacy of the first-person narration in the third-person narration. When he describes a scene, he allows the prose to mimic the thoughts of the protagonist. Being a Dubliner, Joyce suggests, is feeling like both a part of a community as well as an outsider to it. In turn, the narrative arc of the collection, starting with "The Sisters" and ending with "The Dead," invites the reader into Dublin as someone who feels the snow connecting his or her life to others, like Gabriel does, for example, but in remote and cold ways.

The two forms of narration in *Dubliners* also mark a division between stories with young protagonists and stories with adult protagonists. Having the children narrate in first-person, however, produces articulate and eloquent stories, not simplistic, childish action. Other than the fact that these narrators use "I," the language of the earlier stories is almost the same as that of the later stories. Such similarity hints at an equalizing of childhood and adulthood—a person is a Dubliner at all ages. But it also suggests that in adulthood, people lose the affirmative power of directing their own stories. The hope and desire of the Dubliner youth fits with a self-aware "I," whereas the often downtrodden, resigned adults of the later stories, worn out from the hardships of Dublin life, struggle to find their individual voices.

QUESTIONS & ESSAYS

3.   *Discuss the role of story titles in the collection. How does a given title interact with its story and with the titles of other stories? What is the significance of the collection's title?*

Joyce chooses titles that often seem unrelated at the beginnings of stories but deeply symbolic by their conclusions. As such, he requires his readers to make interpretations. With the title of "Two Gallants," for example, the reader expects a story about two gentlemen, but gradually realizes that the protagonists are nothing of the sort. The irony of the title underscores the fact that the story implicitly critiques the lives of Lenehan and Corley, and also suggests the false images that people assign to themselves. Lenehan and Corley probably think themselves to be two gallants, but Joyce shows them to be otherwise. Joyce's choice of titles also serves to create dialogue between the stories. The titles of the opening and closing stories of the collection, for example, could be interchangeable. "The Sisters" fits the content of that story, but it could also appropriately describe the final story, which also involves two aged siblings. Likewise, "The Dead" could serve as the title for the first story, which begins with the anticipation of a death.

Such connections generate a sense of unity in the collection, as well as a circle. By creating titles that intermingle thematically with each other as "The Sisters" and "The Dead" do, Joyce constructs a narrative loop that recalls the circular routines of the lives portrayed in the stories. As such, the title for the collection is significant. These stories depict as well as enact the Dublin life that all of them share. Such circularity defines Joyce's characters, and the title of the collection fixes them to that cycle with the suggestion that life in Dublin, at least for these figures, can be no other way.

SUGGESTED ESSAY TOPICS

1. *Of the fifteen stories in* DUBLINERS, *Joyce focuses on women as protagonists in only four stories, but women appear throughout the collection in various small roles, often in relation to male protagonists. What is the symbolic role of these latter women? Consider particular stories as well as the collection as a whole.*

2. *As the title implies,* DUBLINERS *examines the lives of people in Ireland's capital, and Joyce provides ample geographical details. Since not all readers are familiar with Dublin, such details can be unfamiliar. What purpose, then, do these elements serve?*

3. *Consider the number of deaths, both literal and metaphorical, that occur or are referred to in* DUBLINERS. *Which stories connect through the presence of death, and why is this connection significant?*

4. *Do any stories contain moments in which Joyce's authorial voice and point-of-view seem to speak through the narrators? Use the text to show how this occurs and what Joyce expresses.*

5. *Some stories include a full version of a text cited internally by a character. For example, in "A Painful Case" the reader can examine the article about Mrs. Sinico's death that Mr. Duffy finds, and in "Ivy Day in the Committee Room" the reader can review Hynes's poem about Parnell. What sort of relationship between reader and story do such forms create? What might be Joyce's aim in cultivating this relationship?*

Review & Resources

Quiz

1. In "Araby" the narrator travels to where at the end of the story?

    A. Arabia
    B. Buenos Aires
    C. Nowhere—he stays at home
    D. A bazaar held in Dublin

2. According to the newspaper article in the story, what causes Mrs. Sinico's death in "A Painful Case"?

    A. Old age
    B. Shock or heart failure
    C. Mr. Duffy's political theories
    D. A train accident

3. Which Irish national figure is celebrated in "Ivy Day in the Committee Room"?

    A. James Joyce
    B. Bono
    C. Charles Stuart Parnell
    D. Leopold Bloom

4. What does Maria lose in "Clay"?

    A. Her train ticket
    B. A plum cake
    C. A bundle of clay for Halloween games
    D. Her memory

5. Who narrates "An Encounter"?

    A. A boy named Mangan
    B. Father Flynn
    C. A strange, anonymous man
    D. An unnamed young boy

6. In "A Little Cloud," what does Little Chandler dream about becoming?

    A. A poet
    B. A newspaper reporter in London
    C. A legal copier
    D. A weather forecaster

7. In "The Sisters," what does Father Flynn hold in his hands?

    A. Sherry and biscuits
    B. A bouquet of ivy
    C. A chalice
    D. Nothing

8. What does the narrator liken Eveline to when she freezes on the docks in "Eveline"?

    A. A paralyzed priest
    B. A helpless animal
    C. An angry creature
    D. A brown figure

9. Where is Charles Ségouin from in "After the Race"?

    A. Just outside of Dublin
    B. England
    C. The west of Ireland
    D. France

10. What does Corley procure from his date in "Two Gallants"?

    A. A gold coin
    B. A harp
    C. Fancy cigars
    D. Food

11. What does Miss Ivors call Gabriel when they dance together in "The Dead"?

    A. A poor dancer
    B. A loyal Irishman
    C. A West Briton
    D. A good writer

12. Where does Tom Kernan fall in "Grace"?

    A.   At church
    B.   From a carriage
    C.   From his bed
    D.   Down the stairs at a pub

13. What captures Gretta's attention while the other guests leave the Morkan party in "The Dead"?

    A.   Her husband
    B.   The snow
    C.   Freddy Malins
    D.   A song

14. Who is referred to as "The Madam" in "The Boarding House"?

    A.   Mrs. Kearney
    B.   Mrs. Mooney
    C.   Kate Morkan
    D.   Mangan's sister

15. What does Maria do at the end of "Clay" that makes Joe Donnelly cry?

    A.   She sings a song
    B.   She chooses the plate of clay in the game
    C.   She talks about his brother
    D.   She loses the corkscrew

16. What does Farrington do when he returns home in "Counterparts"?

    A.   He prepares dinner for his wife
    B.   He prays the "Hail Mary"
    C.   He beats his son
    D.   He puts out the fire

17. In "A Painful Case," what does Mr. Duffy see in the park by his house?

    A.   The ghost of Mrs. Sinico
    B.   A newspaper
    C.   Two lovers
    D.   A strange old man

18. In "A Mother," why does Mrs. Kearney storm out of the final concert with her daughter when it is only halfway through?

    A.   She was offended by the nudity
    B.   The piano was out of tune
    C.   The audience booed
    D.   The organizers refused to pay the full fee they'd agreed on

19. Why does Farrington's boss yell at him at the beginning of "Counterparts"?

    A.   He sneaked out of the office to drink a beer
    B.   He failed to complete a copying assignment
    C.   He pawned his boss's watch
    D.   He insulted a client

20. What does Gabriel look at outside of his hotel window in "The Dead"?

    A.   Snow
    B.   A graveyard
    C.   Children playing a game
    D.   Traffic

21. What does Gabriel do in "The Dead" that no one else does during the party meal?

    A.   Eats
    B.   Delivers a speech
    C.   Gets drunk
    D.   Tells a story about his childhood

22. What is one of the words that the boy of "The Sisters" thinks of when he looks through Father Flynn's window?

    A. Begorrah
    B. Corpse
    C. Chalice
    D. Paralysis

23. What sound in "Eveline" suddenly makes Eveline determined to escape her domestic life?

    A. A ship horn
    B. The voice of Frank
    C. A street organ
    D. The voice of her father

24. How does Jimmy Doyle spend all of his money with his friends in "After the Race"?

    A. Betting on car racing
    B. Playing cards
    C. Arm wrestling
    D. Treating his friends to drinks

25. In "A Mother," what does Mrs. Kearney insist her daughter learn, in addition to piano?

    A. The Irish language
    B. The street map of Dublin
    C. Contract law
    D. Irish dance

SUGGESTIONS FOR FURTHER READING

BOSINELLI, ROSA BOLLETTIERI, and HAROLD F. MOSHER, eds.
Rejoycing: New Readings of DUBLINERS. Lexington: University
Press of Kentucky, 1998.

ELLMANN, RICHARD. *James Joyce*. New York: Oxford University
Press, 1982

GARRETT, PETER, ed. *Twentieth Century Interpretations of*
DUBLINERS: *A Collection of Critical Essays*. Englewood Cliffs,
New Jersey: Prentice Hall, 1968.

GIFFORD, DON. *Joyce Annotated: Notes for* DUBLINERS *and* A
PORTRAIT OF THE ARTIST AS A YOUNG MAN. 2nd rev. ed.
Berkeley: University of California Press, 1982.

HERRING, PHILLIP. "DUBLINERS: The Trials of Adolescence." In
James Joyce: A Collection of Critical Essays, edited by Mary T.
Reynolds. Englewood Cliffs, New Jersey: Prentice Hall, 1993.

NORRIS, MARGOT. *Suspicious Readings of Joyce's* DUBLINERS.
Philadelphia: University of Pennsylvania Press, 2003.

TORCHIANA, DONALD T. *Backgrounds for Joyce's* DUBLINERS.
Boston: Allen & Unwin, 1986.